Praise for *Embracing God as Father*

"Writing out of significant personal and pastoral experience, Daniel Bush and Noel Due have drawn on the riches of Scripture and biblical theology to present a captivating portrait of the Father of the Lord Jesus Christ and, thus, of the Father of every believer in Christ. Daniel and Noel's honest, warm-hearted and hope-filled book offers rich encouragement to all who long to experience more of the liberating reality of God as Father."

Rev. Dr. Alistair Wilson
Principal, Dumisani Theological Institute
King William's Town, South Africa

"This book brings blessing because Daniel Bush and Noel Due understand that our adoption by God is more than a doctrine. *Embracing God as Father* opens for us the loving heart of the Father toward his children. God's love then becomes the passion and power forging new spiritual life in believers who live with God as their Father through faith in Christ."

Rev. Josiah Bancroft
Director of Mission, World Harvest Mission
Jenkintown, Pennsylvania

"Here Daniel Bush and Noel Due share, in a pastorally helpful way, great biblical truths that have formed a significant part of their thinking, preaching and teaching throughout years of Christian ministry across several continents. This book should help those who struggle to believe that the Father's love is for them and that he could ever rejoice over them. Through reading this book, may the Father bring you to trust him confidently as Father, and to know the fullness of his joy and love through his Spirit and in his Son."

Rev. Hector Morrison
Principal, Highland Theological College
Dingwall, Scotland

T0035218

"I found *Embracing God as Father* to be deeply challenging. It helped me to see God not just as a distant 'being' but as a Father. I strongly encourage you to read it to better grasp the idea of God as the Father."

Rev. Dr. Suresh Vemulapalli
Director, India Village Ministries
Andhra Pradesh, India

"Arising out of a deep engagement with the Scriptures and a first-hand acquaintance with the transforming love of the triune God, Daniel Bush and Noel Due have written a book that is both theologically rich and deeply personal. Here is a fresh retelling of the old, old story, set in the key signature of the New Testament—that of the Father's eternal purpose to turn lost and needy sinners into his own sons and daughters—that will warm the heart and put strength into weary bones."

Rev. Rob Smith
Lecturer, Sydney Missionary & Bible College
New South Wales, Australia

"If knowing God truly is to know him as he has revealed himself to us, and if knowing God is the essential key to grasping our own identity, then knowing God as he is revealed to us by the Son means the unspeakably great privilege of knowing him as our Father. In Daniel Bush and Noel Due's sensitive, clear and penetrating book, we are brought back to a foundational understanding that we are sons and daughters of the Father because we are his in Christ the Son. When we get this, it changes everything: our worship, the cries of our hearts, our fears, our aims. Knowing the Father and ourselves as his children alters the way we view Christian service, the kind of congregations we develop and the way we present the gospel.

I have seen so many people transformed by the teaching that Daniel and Noel bring, including myself. It has brought rest to my soul and sanity to my ministry. It has taken the anxiety out of my work and has given fresh joy in my marriage. It has altered my conduct of difficult meetings and my approach to people even more awkward than I. It has literally saved lives. I commend this book with the warmest personal appreciation of their long enjoyment and ministry of its message."

Rev. Dominic Smart
Teaching Elder, Gilcomston Church
Aberdeen, Scotland

"Daniel Bush and Noel Due seek to introduce us to the Father they know. They could only say what they say because they know the love of the Father. This book could reshape your faith and your relationships."

Rev. Deane Meatheringham
Minister, Mt. Gambier Uniting Church
South Australia, Australia

"What a treat is offered by this lively, vivid, joyful treatment of our hidden involvement in the life of the triune God! It reclaims something that has been largely lost in our time, the vision of God as the 'prodigal' Father which is granted to all His lost children through His one and only Son. With that too comes the wonderful vision of our participation in His sonship through the ongoing reception of the Holy Spirit, together with every other heavenly blessing, as the Father's provision for us as we hear the gospel and live by faith in His Son. How good it is to be assured that through faith all that belongs to Jesus now belongs to us!"

Rev. Dr. John Kleinig
Prof. Emeritus, Australian Lutheran College
South Australia, Australia

"Daniel Bush and Noel Due's writing is as much a testimony as a technical treatise. At the same time, there is much here which will instruct and which will stimulate our thinking on this great truth of God."

Rev. Dr. Ian Pennicook
Executive Director, New Creation Teaching Ministry
New South Wales, Australia

"God has chosen to reveal Himself in Scripture primarily through metaphor. Arguably no figure impacts us as powerfully as the image of God as Father. Daniel Bush and Noel Due lead the reader through what it means to have God as Father both biblically and from their own experiences."

Rev. Dr. Tom Golding
Principal, Adelaide College of Ministries
South Australia, Australia

Embracing
GOD *as*
FATHER

Philip said to him, "Lord, show us the Father, and it is enough for us." Jesus said to him, "Have I been with you so long, and you still do not know me, Philip? Whoever has seen me has seen the Father."

(John 14:8–9)

Embracing

GOD *as* FATHER

*Christian Identity
in the Family of God*

DANIEL BUSH & NOEL DUE

Foreword by Steve Brown

LEXHAM PRESS

For Our Wives

To Kirsten

Who is this coming up from the wilderness,
Leaning on her beloved?

(Song of Solomon 8:5 NASB)

NSD

To Amy

Have I not commanded you? Be strong and courageous.
Do not be frightened, and do not be dismayed,
for the LORD your God is with you wherever you go.

(Joshua 1:9 ESV)

DJB

Contents

Preface

We never cease to be amazed at how the Father simultaneously orchestrates things on so many levels.

It's been five years since the key event that led to this book occurred. We first met on May 15, 2010; Noel had come from Australia for a teaching and preaching mission in Scotland. That night, he preached a message on Romans 8:1-11—"Slaves Who Fear or Sons Who Cry, 'Father!' "—in Aberdeen, where Dan was living and studying. The themes of Christian identity and the fatherhood of God were so clear and rich that that very night Dan felt strangely led to approach Noel and ask him to consider writing this book. Neither of us knew all that prefaced our chance encounter or anticipated the close friendship and writing partnership that would follow—resulting in the transcription and collaborative reworking of 12 of Noel's sermons into the book that follows. (The sermon noted above became the waters out of which chapter seven emerged.) Helen Keller once said, "Alone we can do so little; together we can do so much." We think she was right!

Sir Isaac Newton wrote, "If I have seen further it is by standing on the shoulders of giants." The turn of phrase predated Newton by a long stretch, and many later echoed the thought. We claim not to have seen further, but simply to have stood on truly gigantic shoulders.

I (Noel) want to acknowledge the debt I owe to two people, above all others. The first is my late wife, Beverley Joy Due, whose middle name so aptly described her character. She was the first person I consciously remember speaking to me of the Father's love, and throughout our more than 30 years together, never lost faith in his care for us and our family. She lived and died in the trust of which this book speaks.

The second is the late preacher G. C. Bingham, whose work on the Fatherhood of God was seminal for so many of us. Those who heard his preaching on the theme and who have read his work will find constant echoes in this volume. May I ask his many friends to attribute any blessing in this volume to him, and any deficiencies to me? In addition, I wish to thank God for others who have written on this topic, not least the late Thomas Smail and P. T. Forsyth, whose timeless works still bless the church today.

I (Dan) acknowledge the shaping influences of the discipleship course, *Sonship* (World Harvest Mission/Serge), created by C. John "Jack" Miller, and the spiritual theology of German Lutheran theologian and preacher Helmut Thielicke. *Sonship* has been extremely formative in my journey to know and trust God as Father. Where this discipleship course laid bare my heart, Thielicke's anthropology and work on identity has had a similar effect on my mind. I am supremely indebted to these "elder brothers" who shared the Lord's work in them so clearly through writing.

This work—and the authors behind it—have also been greatly enriched by the attention of others who have touched this work in a variety of ways—from general comments, to painstaking proofreading and editing, to begging to see the next chapter. We name a few here, but their have been many more:

Deane Meatheringham, Hector Morrison, Nick Needham, Ian Pennicook, Roger Dyer, Douglas Hutcheon, Jim Gordon, Russell Bartlett, Prof. Donald MacLeod, Lee Beckham (who not only proofread the work, but kindly took up the difficult work of authoring the study guide), Marj Wellby (who housed Noel and Kirsten while we worked on much of the first draft), and the team at Lexham Press, especially Abigail Stocker and Brannon Ellis. Thank you, Brannon, for seeing value in this work and desiring a wider audience to benefit from it—we are in your debt.

Lastly, we want to thank the Lord for making Steve Brown so sick during a teaching trip to Washington, DC, that he was essentially forced to cancel his class and remain confined to his hotel room with nothing to do but read an early draft of this book. What a blessed friendship was born out of a horrible cold. Steve, you are a true gift; we know few who live to encourage as you do.

As you now turn from this preface and dive into the book, know that you are not alone. Multitudes have faced heart-wrenching loss, grief, pain, and distress; they too have been pushed into the shadowy valley of which David writes in the 23rd Psalm. We ourselves have traversed that valley, and while our journeys through it have been different, they're strangely similar. The aftermath of such an event is never straightforward, and what it reveals in our hearts, never rosy. *Further deepened by other change and loss, it forces us to face what we dread seeing*—about ourselves, the uncertainty of that in which we trust, and the fragility of relationships and life itself. This is why so many of God's people (typified by Jacob) walk the earth with a limp; he reduces their natural resilience to desperate reliance on grace alone. But it's *there* we find our true identity, crying out even as we experience the Father's embrace. He is so very near in the shadows.

Foreword

My father was a drunk. He was an executive (head of shipping) at a large textile firm with plants in Tennessee, North Carolina, and Holland. He was also an amateur pool hustler who hustled the hustlers who came through our town. He would get a call from the pool hall that there was a new "gun" in town. My father would leave the office, go to the pool hall, and to the surprise of the hustler, leave the pool hall with considerably more cash than he had when he first came in.

"Your daddy," a man told me once, "was the best pool player in western North Carolina when he was sober." I asked the man who was the second best pool player. He laughed and said, "Your daddy when he was drunk."

You may be thinking that my growing years must have been horrible. Actually, you would be wrong. Do you know why? Because my father loved my brother and me with a passionate, unconditional, unrelenting, undeserved, and unreserved love. I wish I had the space to tell you stories; but whether it was in defending us against unjust charges, standing with us when we were "guilty as charged," or showing our pictures to anybody who would look, his love and commitment to us was total. At his funeral, there was a long receiving line, and repeatedly, as people shook our hands, they said, "Do you boys know how much your father loved you?"

Years later when I became a Christian, I was reading the Bible (a book with which I was not yet that familiar) and came across a passage where Jesus said, "Which one of you, if his son asks him for bread, will give him a stone? Or if he asks for a fish, will give him a serpent? If you then, who are evil, know how to give good gifts to your children, how much more will your Father who is in heaven give good things to those who ask him!" (Matt 7:9–11).

I remember the incredible joy with which I received Jesus' words. I remember thinking that if my heavenly Father loved me one fifth as much as my earthly father, I was "good to go." I never had to worry again about my being good enough to please him (he was already pleased because I was his son). I didn't have to worry about my guilt (he knew the bad things about me and loved me anyway). I could trust him with anything (his love would never allow him to be unmerciful, unkind, or angry because I had offended him). In short, both my earthly father and my heavenly one would never say, "I've had it with you."

A lot of years have passed. I thought I would be better than I am by now, but I'm not. I thought I would eventually get to the place where I would be good enough to get my heavenly Father to love me, but it hasn't worked out that way. I thought my knowledge would please him and make him glad he made me his child, but every day, in one way or another, I find out I got it wrong. But God is my Father, and it's okay. He, like my earthly one, never wavers in doing what good fathers do. He never changed and his Fatherhood—his love, mercy, grace and gentle discipline—has been the most important and constant factor in my life.

Reading the book you hold in your hands was not dissimilar to my first reading the words of Jesus about the true nature of a Father who "gives good things" to his children. As I read, I was overwhelmed again by a heavenly Father who revealed himself to us in Jesus. I found myself sometimes moved to tears and sometimes laughing the laughter of the free and loved.

Read this book and rejoice in your Father!

Steve W. Brown

Introduction

God knows what we really need, as a good Father should. Sometimes we find ourselves overcome with uncertainty, anxiety, and fear. At times we feel that all is dark, all the time. We're often perplexed, frequently confused, and commonly puzzled, not just by the events that happen to us and to others, but by the sin and sadness in our own hearts. Our spirits yearn to know that there's something else out there, that events aren't random, that we haven't been abandoned. In truth, there is Someone else—above and beyond, but at the same time inexpressibly close. Even in darkness so close we can feel it, God our Father is closer. He's never absent, but is actively supplying what we need, when we need it. In the words of a friend's song,

> When all around is sin and pain,
> And death is near and life is vain,
> Then glory breaks from out the tomb,
> As new life issues from its womb,
> And we are caught to Thee on high,
> Where strong, strong Love can never die.[1]

Deuteronomy 32:39 says it's God who wounds and God who sustains and heals. He wounds and heals, but not how we might think. He's the one who gives life and who takes his beloved children home to himself, by whatever means and in whatever time he chooses. Yet his wounding is never arbitrary—we need not recoil from him in fear. His is a beautiful, sacred wounding that brings new life and refreshed knowledge of his love. In other words, God often brings his love and grace in the context of suffering and pain, in the midst of circumstances that perplex and frustrate our human efforts at achieving comfort and control. Throughout the Bible, our Father is the one who comes, in grace, to the weak, the broken, the lost, the grief-stricken, the sinful, the alienated, the despised, the exiled, and the lonely. And so if this is where you are, this book is for you.

This book isn't for those who have it all together, who assume that the Christian life will be free of suffering or pain. For me (Noel), sitting with my wife until terminal cancer had run its course disabused me of that expectation; the pain still resurfaces even now, for grief isn't like the common cold—unpleasant for a while, but over quickly enough. When times are good and we feel relatively untroubled, it's easy to have a feel-good "God" whom we smile at as a sort of fairy God-father who meets all our felt needs (not necessarily our real needs). But it's in times of deep suffering that our heavenly Father's true love becomes ever more richly known to us. Through times of trial and difficulty, we discover we don't have an indulgent God-father, but rather the *awesome* God of Abraham, Isaac, and Jacob—our Shepherd, Savior, and Lord. It is *this* almighty God and Father who lavishes his affection on us in good times and bad.

The great reality of God's fatherhood is one of the most wonderful treasures we can ever come to know. And coming to know it deeply is at the heart of exploring the fullness of our sonship. Our hope for you as you read this book is not that you would come to understand God's fatherhood in only an academic way (though, particularly in the first sections, you may not *immediately* see the relevance of all that's said). Rather, our hope is that you might know that the Father himself actually comes to us and lavishes his providential care upon us, and, in that special knowing of the heart, grasp a glimpse of his love for us as his dear sons and daughters.

Our Father in His Son

The very good news of this book is that God is not like our earthly fathers. At the center of distinctly Christian theology lies the doctrine of the Trinity. While God is one essence or being, the Father, the Son, and the Holy Spirit are three distinct persons. God is *tri-une*, "Three in One." When God acts, the whole of the triune Godhead acts: to create, redeem, glorify, heal, and so on. But in terms of person and function, each maintains his distinctiveness. Each person has his own personal identity and way of performing the unified works of God. This being the case, the Father can be seen to be the first person of the Godhead. The Father isn't first in terms of being or time (since God is one and eternal), but in terms of his personal relationship to his "only-begotten" Son (John 1:18) and the Spirit who "proceeds" from him together with the Son (John 15:26). The Father is likewise first in the initiation of all God's works. So when God the Father creates, he does so through his Son, by the agency of the Spirit. Likewise, when the Father redeems, he does so in the sending of the Son, who took upon himself our humanity, in the power of the Spirit (Gen 1:1-3; John 1:1-3, 14).

All of this might sound a bit academic, but it's really important. For as this book focuses on God as Father, by no means are we diminishing the glory, dignity, or honor of the Son and the Spirit. The truth is: *It's only possible for the Father to be all in all if the Son is Lord of all.* The Father himself delights that the Son is glorified, and the Son and the Spirit delight that the Father is exalted. The Father gives the Son lordship over the whole creation, and the Son's lordship resounds to the praise of the

Father's glory. The Son is known to be Lord of all because the Father has sent his Spirit into the world to proclaim the victory that Jesus won in the cross and resurrection. He is our high priest, the leader of our worship, and the one through whom the Spirit is poured out. The Spirit comes to glorify the Father and the Son, to take all that is theirs and reveal it to us. What must be absolutely clear as we continue is that the glory of God is glorious in and through all the Persons, who delight in their complete unity. And through the humanity of Jesus, they open themselves to us, that we may find our home in the Father's household (see John 14–17).

The doctrine of the Trinity also means that there was never a time when the Father has not been Father. He didn't become the Father when Jesus was born. Everything he has ever done, he has done as the true Father. He has ever been the Father of the eternal Son sent by the Father to take our humanity to himself in order to save us (Luke 1:35; John 1:14; Rev 13:8). Creation and redemption are both gifts from him, and in him we find that the whole of human history, from creation through redemption to final glory, reaches its goal. Emphasizing the fullness of our relationship with the Father actually establishes—rather than excludes or diminishes—the glory of each person of our glorious triune God.

Living in Present Hope

As we more fully learn to see God as Father and ourselves as his sons and daughters through Jesus, we also learn to *wait* for the full revealing of our destiny. Our waiting isn't in vain. The outcome we look forward to isn't in question; it's sure and certain. Even though labor pains are great, and they increase in intensity, doesn't this tell us that delivery is assured? The Lord will accomplish what he's proclaimed. Jesus will be Lord of all—he is already, but he will be seen and acknowledged as such by all. Consider the following passages of Scripture:

Psalm 22:27–29:

> All the ends of the earth shall remember
>   and turn to the Lord,
> and all the families of the nations
>   shall worship before you.
> For kingship belongs to the Lord,
>   and he rules over the nations.
> All the prosperous of the earth eat and worship;
>   before him shall bow all who go down to the dust,
>   even the one who could not keep himself alive.

Isaiah 45:22–23:

> Turn to me and be saved,
>   all the ends of the earth!
>   For I am God, and there is no other.
> By myself I have sworn;
>   from my mouth has gone out in righteousness
>   a word that shall not return:
> "To me every knee shall bow,
>   every tongue shall swear allegiance."

Acts 10:34–36 NKJV:

> Then Peter opened his mouth and said: "In truth I perceive that God shows no partiality. But in every nation whoever fears Him and works righteousness is accepted by Him. The word which God sent to the children of Israel, preaching peace through Jesus Christ—He is Lord of all."

Romans 14:10–11:

> Why do you pass judgment on your brother? Or you, why do you despise your brother? For we will all stand before the judgment seat of God; for it is written,

> "As I live, says the Lord, every knee shall bow to me,
>   and every tongue shall confess to God."

Philippians 2:9–11:

> Therefore God has highly exalted him and bestowed on
> him the name that is above every name, so that at the
> name of Jesus every knee should bow, in heaven and on
> earth and under the earth, and every tongue confess
> that Jesus Christ is Lord, to the glory of God the Father.

There's no doubt that Jesus will lead the whole creation in worship, to the glory of the Father. There's no doubt that those in Christ will be conformed to his image. And there's no doubt that God the Father will be all in all.

And so embracing sonship is also waiting with eager expectancy for what God has promised—this is the New Testament meaning of hope. It's not *wishing* for something that might possibly be; it's *waiting* for that which must inevitably be—since, in one sense, it *already is.* God has already established our hope's solid rock, which is Christ: "So this is what the Sovereign LORD says: 'See, I lay a stone in Zion, a tested stone, a precious cornerstone for a sure foundation; the one who trusts will never be dismayed' " (Isaiah 28:16). True hope isn't hanging on to see if God will triumph; it's waiting in expectant faith to see the triumph of God revealed. This theme runs as a river through this book. That we have a Father to whom we look; to whom we cry out in prayer; and whom we wait upon in hope are crucial to understanding Christian sonship.

Children in Distress

In this present phase of the Father's plan, however, this glorious hope seems a distant dream. We're often storm-tossed in depths of deep darkness and suffering. Sometimes—God's children though we are—we wonder about the point of it all; troubles that come in an overwhelming flood can cause us to long for our earthly life to cease. Great biblical characters have known the same experience (e.g., Job 3:3, 11–12; Jer 15:10; 20:14–18). Many of us can join David in saying, "I am weary with my moaning;

every night I flood my bed with tears; I drench my couch with my weeping. My eye wastes away because of grief; it grows weak because of all my foes" (Psa 6:6–7).

Yet, the brilliant light of the Father's own promises comes breaking through the clouds of darkness, not just the first time but every time we turn to him: He has certified that there is no condemnation for us; that there will be no separation from his love; and that through the depths he is there with us—not only caring and comforting, but *conforming* us to the image of his Son (Rom 8:28–29). Our sonship is also marked by him being at work for us and within us. And ultimately, the final resurrection will be our Father's affirmation before the whole of creation, to all the unseen spiritual powers and principalities, that his sons and daughters are indeed pleasing to him and loved by him.

God is at work through the trials and turmoil to fashion our hearts in the image of his dear Son. Far too quickly, however, we can become like Job's comforters, who drew direct lines between Job's suffering and God's judgment on sin. We too easily, and quite wrongly, draw direct lines from suffering to punishment. We do it to ourselves; we do it even more readily to others. But our sonship should remind us that in Jesus there's no condemnation and no separation from God, our Father. When it seems as though joy has fled forever, our security in all things at all times lies outside of ourselves in Jesus. In him we know we're the beloved children of our Father. As sons and daughters of God, we have Christ as our head and our hope. In him we know the glory of the Father. In him we're assured of the Father's love, and by the good news of his free grace we're transformed into those who freely and joyfully trust him and love him in return. This is perhaps what grasping the reality of our sonship is all about.

The Power of a New Affection

The great Scottish preacher Thomas Chalmers, in his sermon "The Expulsive Power of a New Affection," said this about true spiritual transformation:

Salvation by grace—salvation by free grace—salvation not of works, but according to the mercy of God—salvation on such a footing is not more indispensable to the deliverance of our persons from the hand of justice, than it is to the deliverance of our hearts from the chill and the weight of ungodliness. *Retain a single shred or fragment of legality with the gospel, and we raise a topic of distrust between man and God. We take away from the power of the gospel to melt and to conciliate. For this purpose, the freer it is, the better it is.* That very peculiarity which so many dread as the germ of antinomianism, is, in fact, the germ of a new spirit, and a new inclination against it. Along with the light of a free gospel, does there enter the love of the gospel, which, in proportion as we impair the freeness, we are sure to chase away. And never does the sinner find within himself so mighty a moral transformation, as when, under the belief that he is saved by grace, he feels constrained thereby to offer his heart a devoted thing, and to deny ungodliness.

To do any work in the best manner, we should make use of the fittest tools for it.[2]

The language is old and perhaps difficult to follow (after all, it was preached over 150 years ago), but the issues he wrestled with are always present: Only in the full, free, grace-filled, and God-given revelation of God's own love in Jesus are our hearts free from the sinful attractions which bind and destroy us. Even more, Chalmers was convinced that the power of this new affection of the heart lies in the very freedom of God's love—in its lavishness and its abundant grace. We can never be sure and settled in his love for us when we think our relationship with God is legalistic (i.e., we get what we earn) or when we think our Father's affection for us is conditional (which drives legalism deep into us). We're subject to a restless conscience and to the suspicion that God isn't *for* us unless we earn his favor and keep ourselves in it.

This treadmill does more than rob us of spiritual vitality and joy—it denies our very sonship. If we don't see and believe ourselves to be *loved completely by God through Jesus*, then distrust will create a chasm in our relationship with God, which the flesh, the world, and the devil will fill with fear. And when our hearts are filled with fear, our relationship with the Father becomes something we toil at in self-justification rather than receive as a gift of grace. When Christianity becomes imbued with legalism, it's not real Christianity. As the Apostle John says, "Fear has to do with punishment, and whoever fears has not been perfected in love" (1 John 4:18). What will be unveiled at the last day is the fullness of the love with which *we have already been loved*, from the One who is Love (1 John 4:8). What we'll know *then* is the revelation of a love we have *now* in Jesus.

"[I]f anyone is in Christ, he is a new creation," writes Paul. "The old has passed away; behold, the new has come" (2 Cor 5:17). "From now on, therefore, we regard no one according to the flesh" (2 Cor 5:16). Don't judge yourself according to the flesh; don't judge one another any longer according to the old nature that has passed away. In Christ, God has ransomed, healed, restored, and forgiven you. *Christ has already revealed in his work what God thinks of you.* This is the expulsive power of a new affection. By focusing on this—on how the Father sees us in Christ—we are owning our sonship and leaving behind the nagging fear stirred up by the devil, the world, and our own sin.

In this current phase of history between the first and second appearing of the Lord Jesus that the Bible calls "the last days" (Heb 1:2), our hearts are as conflicted as the world around us. We face powerful forces bringing constant accusation with the sole object of driving us into fear. *The fear of all fears is the loss of God's love and favor.* We fear being abandoned by him. We fear that our sin will cause him, or has already caused him, to write us out of his book. We fear that we'll reap God's punishment after all—though Jesus took it for us, doesn't the accuser remind us that we still deserve it? In this conflict often our main motivation isn't love, but self-protection and self-justification. How often do we look at a Christian brother or sister and become unsettled by our own fearful insecurity? It's so easy to adopt a critical attitude or a negative judgmentalism that sees only faults and failures. A harsh view of others deflects away from ourselves the shame and guilt we feel in our own hearts.

But, in Jesus, we're fully reconciled to one another as well as to the Father. As sons and daughters, we're also brothers and sisters. Together we've been granted every spiritual blessing in Christ. Nothing is lacking. All who are in Christ have been made complete (Col 2:10). No one is more loved than another; each is loved perfectly in a redeeming grace that has accounted for every failure as well as every all-too-imperfect "success."

On the last day, when God will be all in all, we will not only believe but *see* that this really is the case. We will see one another as we really are—in Christ. We will know ourselves fully loved in him, and we will love the Father's family fully and without hindrance since we will all be filled with the Father's own fullness. This is heaven. There will be no envy, bitterness, jealousy, or unforgiveness. We will see one another in Jesus and rejoice in the fullness of each other's sonship, just as God rejoices in ours.

A Personal Embrace

This book will help you to know what God the Father has done in giving his greatest gift, in making himself our Father in and through Jesus, his Son. "Whoever has seen me has seen the Father" (John 14:9)—so Father and Son are one in their love and joy and desire to bless. God sends his Spirit into our hearts to teach us this love and to enable us to call upon God as our Father (John 14:16–17; Gal 4:6). This book can't do this for you. But it can tell you what God the Father has done, is doing, and does every day as he speaks his Word into our hearts. This book won't continuously speak about Christian sonship, either—but it *will* focus on the one whose sons and daughters we are. So our hope is that as we meditate upon God's Word, by the Holy Spirit, that you'll not just *learn* about God's fatherhood, but *experience* it with confidence and joy.

CHAPTER 1

God the Father: All in All

The universal question, "What's the purpose of my life?," might well be rephrased, "What am I waiting for?" Many have commented on life's meaning and purpose. The brilliantly succinct answer of the Westminster Shorter Catechism, that our "chief end is to glorify God, and to enjoy him forever," is often quoted because it sums up the Bible's teaching so well. Yet as true as this is, we rarely understand it in terms of children longing to delight in God as our Father and to bring him joy *by enjoying him* now and forever. So this is where we will begin.

Consider the following passage from Paul:

> Christ has been raised from the dead, the firstfruits of those who have fallen asleep. For as by a man came death, by a man has come also the resurrection of the dead. For as in Adam all die, so also in Christ shall all be made alive. But each in his own order: Christ the first-fruits, then at his coming those who belong to Christ. Then comes the end, when he delivers the kingdom to

God the Father after destroying every rule and every authority and power. For he must reign until he has put all his enemies under his feet. The last enemy to be destroyed is death. For "God has put all things in subjection under his feet." But when it says, "all things are put in subjection," it is plain that he is excepted who put all things in subjection under him. When all things are subjected to him, then the Son himself will also be subjected to him who put all things in subjection under him, that God may be all in all (1 Cor 15:20–28).

The conclusion of the present phase of history isn't, according to Paul, the absolute end of history. A new endless phase will commence with Jesus' return. And with his second coming Jesus will give back to the Father the kingdom he has been given by the Father (1 Cor 15:24), subjecting himself to the Father so that "God may be all in all" (1 Cor 15:28). Philippians makes the same point: "At the name of Jesus every knee should bow, in heaven and on earth and under the earth, and every tongue confess that Jesus Christ is Lord, to the glory of God the Father" (2:10–11). And so the end and goal of human history isn't some abstract glorification of God, but the joyous glorification of God the Father in Jesus Christ our Lord.

Back to the Beginning

The end of history is oriented to the Father because it has been so since the beginning. Paul declared to the philosophers of Athens, "The God who made the world and everything in it, being Lord of heaven and earth, does not live in temples made by man, nor is he served by human hands, as though he needed anything, since he himself gives to all mankind life and breath and everything" (Acts 17:24–25). And quoting one of their own ancient poets he tells them we're all "his offspring," that "in him we live and move and have our being" (Acts 17:28). We were brought into being for the purpose of knowing and enjoying the Creator as our Father.

While all humanity has one Father, the sad reality is that they're not all his sons and daughters in the way they were created to be. Thus, Paul calls even the learned and worldly-wise to "repent" from their ignorance of the truth about God revealed in Jesus' redeeming work (Acts 17:30).

Created as God's son (Luke 3:38), Adam with his wife gave life to all who descended from them. We are all their descendants, but we have "descended" in another sense, too: We've fallen away from the truth of our original blessedness. The knowledge of God as Father has been lost through sin, corruption, and rebellion (Rom 1:18–32) with the result that we've turned in on ourselves, seeking to meet our own desires at the expense of others. We're at war first with ourselves and with our unmet desires, and then we're at war with each other as we seek to use each other to meet those desires. No wonder we're trapped in a cycle of complaining, grumbling, fighting, and forcing! Strife on a global scale has its origin in the loss of the knowledge of God our Father.

Yet the truth of the matter is that only in the recovery of that knowledge, only in a wholly dependent relationship with God the Father through his Son, are we whole and our desires met. This is quite different from what bare human reason tells us, because it's not something we know instinctively. In fact, there's nothing we can look at in the world by which to know this. Even the crucifixion is ambiguous; its meaning isn't on the surface to be grasped by sight. Only in personal encounter with the Lord himself are our eyes blessed with faith. This happened to the disciples when they met the risen Lord in the upper room, and it happens to us when we're overcome and undone by meeting him in his Word.

But our point is the world doesn't see it. It can't because such things are discerned by faith. It doesn't see God's free initiative to enter into the world in Jesus to restore our knowledge of his love for us and, in that love, to define who we are and to heal our "self-esteem" from its ultimate bankruptcy. The world thinks it defines itself—that it gives itself meaning, hope, and security.

As it goes about defining, making, and securing itself, it's actually about the business of destroying itself. We aren't self-defining creatures. God defines our meaning and existence. He gives us the deepest meaning and the highest honor of being his own children. And so the end of human history has the beginning—God and his purposes for creation—as its aim.

In the end, the Father's children shall be revealed and all creation will rejoice and be glorified (Rom 8:18-25). If you really reflect on this it will be a breath of fresh air, a sigh of relief. You can relax, rest, and trust him with each and every aspect of your life, every circumstance, for everything is moving towards this glorious end. God the Father is the goal to which things are headed (Eph 1:3-14), and he desires that we know him as this end for ourselves. Oh, that we would not search out other "chief ends," but that we would begin now to glorify him by finding our highest enjoyment in him, in who he is for us!

Securing History's Hope

All we've said so far must be understood in the context of hope in the fulfillment of God's promises. From the beginning—as soon as sin caused our loss of knowledge of God as Father—God was right there as the loving Father promising redemption through an "offspring" who would defeat the serpent and rescue his people (Gen 3:15). Later, God appeared to Abraham making the same promise to him, to his descendants, and through him to the nations of the earth (Gen 22:17-18; Gal 3:16). The promise was renewed with Isaac and then Jacob, David and then Solomon. All of God's dealings with his children occur in the context of these various covenant promises, which have at their heart the one promise of the coming Messiah.

Our experience of hope and our experience of being the Father's sons and daughters are closely related. Hope comes in fixing ourselves to his covenant promises, believing what we hear rather than what we see, expectantly waiting on God. We don't hope in hope itself, but in its promised fulfillment.

God's promises have always anticipated deliverance from all that's blocked us from knowing ourselves as the object of the Father's affection—the blockage is the sin of our own hard hearts. It keeps us from seeing God and ourselves rightly, from knowing ourselves to be his beloved children. We can't secure our own hope. Hope is secured by promise.

In 1 Corinthians 15:20-28, Paul addresses the destiny and glory of humanity and also the whole creation. All things are now subject to the risen Jesus. While in the first Adam, the creation came into chaotic disharmony and dislocation, in the last Adam, all is set right. In presenting this finished work to the Father, Jesus does what the first Adam was created to do, but failed. In presenting us to the Father, we find our hope secured by Jesus' person and work, outside of ourselves and on our behalf. Jesus is himself the fulfillment of God's promises, and in him our dignity and destiny is fully sealed.

Firstfruits of the Harvest

Because of this, in 1 Corinthians 15:20, 23, Paul calls Jesus the "firstfruits." Firstfruits are the early sampling, the first ripe produce, of a larger harvest yet to come. Naturally, they share the same nature and character as the rest of the crop of which they're a part. The firstfruits are also considered the choicest part of the harvest (the priests of Israel frequently used them in sacrificial offerings at the temple). If the firstfruits are good, so will the rest of the harvest be. In these ways, the firstfruits represent the whole crop and are the guarantee of the quality of the harvest to come.

On a trip I (Noel) once took to India, I came across a sweet, spicy dessert called "first rice." It goes by this name because it's made from the early, choice portion of the rice crop. The first rice is taken to be an accurate indicator of the nature and quality of the coming harvest. When the time is right and the farmers go back to the fields for the rest of the rice, they don't expect to find watermelons! They expect to find rice, and rice of a particular quality. The firstfruits is the guarantee of what the rest of the harvest will be like.

So when Jesus is said to be the firstfruits of those raised from the dead, we're to understand that Jesus was raised from the dead on our behalf, as both the forerunner and representative head of an entirely new humanity. He was raised as the head of a new harvest, every part of which will be of the same character that he is. As Paul says a little later in the chapter, "Just as we have borne the image of the man of dust, we shall also bear the image of the man of heaven" (1 Cor 15:49). As surely as we're children of Adam by nature, by grace we'll be conformed to the image of the Son of God (Rom 8:29).

This is why in so many places Paul uses the phrases "in Christ," "with Christ," "through Christ," and so on, to describe our new status and character. These describe our inseparable union with Jesus. Because he's our firstfruits, we're granted participation with him in the relational beauty and fullness that he knows as the beloved Son of the Father. He's the guarantee of the character of our glorified humanity in the coming resurrection.

Jesus' resurrection is the promise and guarantee of our resurrection. It's important to recognize that Paul speaks in two ways about the resurrection. Here, in 1 Corinthians 15, the apostle is speaking about the resurrection of our physical bodies on the last day. But in other places he speaks about a resurrection that has already occurred:

> God, being rich in mercy, because of the great love with which he loved us, even when we were dead in our trespasses, made us alive together with Christ—by grace you have been saved—and raised us up with him and seated us with him in the heavenly places in Christ Jesus (Eph 2:4-6).

This resurrection is essentially a comment about our spiritual condition and relationship with God. We have been raised up with Christ, and in Christ we have been made alive from the dead. But we still await a resurrection body to match our new status.

Our earthly bodies—mortal and perishable as they are—must yet be transformed to match our new status as sons of God in Jesus.

When this final resurrection takes place, we'll be fully transformed into what we already are: righteous and holy in Christ, members of the last Adam, redeemed from the death of the first Adam. Our destiny is the destiny of Jesus Christ: to be raised with him, to be seated with him, and to rule with him everlastingly as a kingdom of priests to our God and Father. We enter the presence of God by virtue of our union with Christ. We know the Father in and through him. In him, we are filled with the Father, who becomes all in all to us.

Citizens of Heaven

Paul says that "our citizenship is in heaven, and from it we await a savior, the Lord Jesus Christ, who will transform our lowly body to be like his glorious body, by the power that enables him even to subject all things to himself" (Phil 3:20–21). Undoubtedly this passage is speaking about the resurrection that will occur on the last day. And yet even though we wait in anticipation of this glorious new beginning, we are no less sons and daughters of God now, in the present. For in this interim period we have already received the gift of adoption, we are already blessed with the Spirit of God who teaches our hearts to cry, "Abba! Father!" (Gal 4:6). In a very real sense, the new creation is already upon us. If anyone is in Christ, there is a new creation (2 Cor 5:17)!

And yet in this period of expectant waiting, we know much turmoil and pain. Often we don't feel as though there's any newness or comfort for us. And yet Paul wrote: "For I consider that the sufferings of this present time are not worth comparing with the glory that is to be revealed to us" (Rom 8:18). How can he have said this? How is it that he could look so resolutely beyond the difficulties and wait so patiently? Because of the new hope that permeated his heart, which we catch a glimpse of just a few verses later:

For we know that the whole creation has been groaning together in the pains of childbirth until now. And not only the creation, but we ourselves, who have the first-fruits of the Spirit, groan inwardly as we wait eagerly for adoption as sons, the redemption of our bodies. For in this hope we were saved. Now hope that is seen is not hope. For who hopes for what he sees? But if we hope for what we do not see, we wait for it with patience (Rom 8:22–25).

As those who belong to Christ, we live safely enclosed between two great promises proclaimed by Paul:

There is therefore now no condemnation for those who are in Christ Jesus (Rom 8:1).

For I am sure that neither death nor life, nor angels nor rulers, nor things present nor things to come, nor powers, nor height nor depth, nor anything else in all creation, will be able to separate us from the love of God in Christ Jesus our Lord (Rom 8:38–39).

This is where you live as a Christian. We live between the great reality that in Christ there's no condemnation, and in him we never know any separation from the love of God.

The Father All in All

Many a spouse has heard their partner say something like, "You mean the world to me." But this isn't what Paul is getting at when he writes that the Father will be all in all. While we don't want to minimize the overwhelming and heartfelt endearment expressed, "Ah, you mean the world to me, Father" doesn't plumb the depths of the reality of God being all in all. Such a feeling will surely be present, but Paul is saying something more and different from this. He's saying not that the Father will mean all to all, but that he will be all in all. In other words, the Father will fill those who are in Christ in the same relational fullness that

Christ himself has with the Father. This doesn't mean, of course, that the Son becomes the Father—each of the divine persons is eternally distinct in their oneness. But it does mean that everything that the Father has belongs to Jesus, and we belong to him (Eph 1:23). And by virtue of our union with Christ by faith, we will also attain to "the measure of the stature of the fullness of Christ" (Eph 4:13). That is, as Christ is filled with the Father, we will be also.

So what does this really mean? Let's be honest, to be filled to the fullness of God the Father does sound somewhat peculiar. Let me suggest that the meaning is easier to grasp than it sounds.

The Bible tells us that God is love (1 John 4:8), that the Son is his beloved (Luke 3:22; Col 1:12, literally, "the son of his love"), and that the Spirit pours the love of God the Father into our hearts (Rom 5:5; Gal 4:6). Hence to be filled to the fullness of God the Father, to have him be all in all, means that in the end the love of the Father prevails in us. In other words, he will bring us to a maturity of knowledge—head and heart—of his love for us that is so complete that the entirety of our being and character will be utterly and exclusively shaped by it. And if we'll recall, this is exactly the fulfillment of the greatest commandment: "Love the Lord your God with all your heart and with all your soul and with all your mind" (Matt 22:37).

God, who is love, will fill us with his love through the Spirit in the Son. Every part of us will be attuned to the holy love that he is. Every element of our being, in every form and part, will be "full." This means that there will be no room for us to be filled with a host of other things that are at cross purposes with his love, such as anxiety, frustration, discontentment, unthankfulness, pride, selfishness, impatience, irritability, lack of self-control, anger, judgmentalism, envy, jealousy, and on and on. To be filled is to be fulfilled. Being totally mature in the knowledge of God's perfect love for us will cast out all fear (1 John 4:18) and fill our hearts with a perfect reflexive love for the Father.

Paul had to criticize the Corinthian church about their judg-mentalism, their lack of patience, and their self-exalting way of relating to one another. But the basis of Paul's critique is the future hope we've been speaking of. In reality, this future hope is already present and fully ours in Christ. We've been blessed with every spiritual blessing in him. But we don't live in the full-ness of it now. That awaits the resurrection at the last day and the transformation of our bodies in glory. But, because what we will be is in fact what we are now by faith, Paul in effect says, "Look, this is what it's all going to be. We possess faith, hope, and love, and the greatest of these is love. So live now in the light of who you are, and who you're going to be" (1 Cor 13). This indeed is the fulfillment of all the commandments (e.g., Matt 22:37-40; Gal 5:13-15; cf. Gal 5:22-23; Rom 13:8-10), because God is love.

In Christ, every man and woman is completely and utterly loved by the Father. Even the pain and tragedy, the loss and be-reavement, and the deep suffering that sometimes fills us with perplexity and confusion—all this is finally from love and for love. In the end we'll see that it has been so, and that it could have been no other way. The God who is love was love from before the foundation of the world. In his love he has planned to fill us with himself that his joy may be full in us and that we might be filled in him. This love for us is from before the world's foundations were laid, which means it was for us even while we hated God and were hostile towards him. In fact, it's this love of God that's responsible for converting our hearts to him. He has taken ac-count of every single one of our sinful thoughts and evil deeds, and cleansed us by the judgment of the cross.

The fullness of love that we await on the last day is not a new love but the complete revelation—the full unveiling to our sight—of the love that's been given to us in Christ. God's love is at work here, now. So ultimately the question is not "For what do we wait?" but "For whom?" For whom do we wait? We wait for God to fully reveal his grace and mercy in Christ, for the time when God the Father will be all in all.

CHAPTER 2

Filled with Fullness

The resurrection of the dead weighed heavily upon the mind of the Apostle Paul in 1 Corinthians 15. There he speaks about the resurrection of Jesus and about the resurrection awaiting us specifically because Jesus' resurrection has already occurred. He says, "But in fact Christ has been raised from the dead, the firstfruits of those who have fallen asleep" (15:20).

As we observed in the last chapter, firstfruits is a magnificent metaphor since it relates to the Old Testament practice of bringing in the first part of the harvest and carries with it a couple of very important ideas.

Firstly, the firstfruits of the harvest is the *guarantee* of what is to come. In ancient Israel, a celebratory gathering known as the Feast of Harvest was held when the firstfruits were gathered. Because of the harvest celebration in Jerusalem, a host of international pilgrims were present to hear the gospel being preached on the day of Pentecost, as it was then called. The first believers were the firstfruits of the harvest of the nations, a gospel harvest "in Jerusalem and in all Judea and Samaria, and to the ends of the earth" (Acts 1:8). Yet there's another harvest yet to come, which is implicit in the concept of firstfruits. Pentecost marked the beginning of the great ingathering that would continue throughout the world and culminate in the appearing of Jesus at the last day. In other words, what Paul is saying is Jesus' resurrection is the *guarantee* that the Father's full harvest will be gathered in.

Secondly, the firstfruits indicate the quality of the harvest to come. As the farmers took the firstfruits of the barley, they learned the character and quality of the later harvest—the point being, if Jesus is the firstfruits of those who have fallen asleep in him, then they will be of the same character and quality as he is. The quality of *our* resurrected life is thereby guaranteed by virtue of *his*.

Paul puts the entire matter most emphatically, and we may take it as a promise.

> But in fact Christ has been raised from the dead, the firstfruits of those who have fallen asleep. For as by a man came death, by a man has come also the resurrection of the dead. For as in Adam all die, so also in Christ shall all be made alive. But each in his own order: Christ the firstfruits, then at his coming those who belong to Christ. Then comes the end, when he delivers the kingdom to *God the Father* (1 Cor 15:20-24a).

The question of whether we are emphasizing the fatherhood of God too much could be legitimately asked. Might such an emphasis diminish the role of the Holy Spirit or of Jesus as Lord? In effect, Paul's answer to the question is, no. Notice what he says in the section following what we've just quoted.

> Then comes the end, when he [that is Jesus Christ] delivers the kingdom to God the Father after destroying every rule and every authority and power. For he must reign until he has put all his enemies under his feet (1 Cor 15:24-25).

That is, God the Father must reign until he has put Jesus' en-emies, which are also the Father's, under his feet, the last enemy being death itself (1 Cor 15:26). The passage continues:

> For "God has put all things in subjection under his feet." But when it says, "all things are put in subjection," it is plain that he is excepted who put all things in sub-jection under him. When all things are subjected to him (15:27–28a).

It's the Father who's subjecting all things to his Son. And once this has conclusively occurred, when all things are subject to the Son, "then the Son himself will also be subjected to him who put all things in subjection under him, that God [the Father] may be all in all" (15:28b). All of this is very similar in a way to what Paul says in Philippians:

> Therefore God has highly exalted him and bestowed on him the name that is above every name, so that at the name of Jesus every knee should bow, in heaven and on earth and under the earth, and every tongue con-fess that Jesus Christ is Lord, to the glory of God the Father (2:9–11).

The goal of Jesus' sonship and his being raised as the first-fruits of the dead means that the Father is all in all, to him and to those raised in him. To put it another way, God's goal was that in Jesus men and women would be filled with the Father himself. The manifestation of this "fullness of the Father" in our lives is our concern in this chapter.

Not Like Our Fathers

Human fatherhood is always flawed. No human father is sinless. But even if we "who are evil, know how to give good gifts to [our] children, how much more will [our] Father who is in heaven give good things to those who ask him!" (Matt 7:11). It's not a question, but an assertive statement. The Father is more willing to give than we can imagine. One of the greatest expositions of God's action towards us is found in the opening chapter of Ephesians. "Blessed be the God and Father of our Lord Jesus Christ," says Paul (Eph 1:3). The rest of his letter, and especially the paragraphs following 1:3, are governed by the action of God the Father. In fact, in the original Greek text, 1:3 all the way to 1:14 is a single sentence, carrying as its subject "God and Father of our Lord Jesus Christ." Thus, everything in this long sentence tells us what our God and Father has done. He has blessed us (1:3), chosen us (1:4), predestined us (1:5), adopted us (1:5), bestowed upon us (1:6), redeemed us (1:7), forgiven us (1:7), lavished on us (1:8), made known to us (1:9), worked all things to the counsel of his will (1:11), and sealed us (1:13).

The Father is the subject, but we're the object of those verbs. A stunning thought, isn't it, that the Father should be so fixated on us that his whole plan and purpose is towards us and for us? Paul understood this intensely, and this is why in the midst of cataloging God's action towards us he can't help but break into prayer:

> I do not cease to give thanks for you, remembering you in my prayers, that the God of our Lord Jesus Christ, the Father of glory, may give you a spirit of wisdom and of revelation in the knowledge of him, having the eyes of your hearts enlightened, that you may know what is the hope to which he has called you, what are the riches of his glorious inheritance in the saints, and what is the immeasurable greatness of his power toward us who believe, according to the working of his great might that he worked in Christ when he raised him from the dead and seated him at his right hand in the heavenly places, far above all rule and authority and power and dominion, and above every name that is named, not only in this age but also in the one to come. And he put all things under his feet and gave him as head over all

things to the church, which is his body, the fullness of
him who fills all in all (Eph 1:16–23).

There is a lot packed into this prayer. But notice the marvel-
ous thing that Paul tucks away at its end. We sometimes think
that Jesus is the head of the Church, and this is true—the Church
is his body, and he is its head. But Paul is saying something different and more expansive here. He is saying that Jesus has been
given as head over all things *to the Church*. In other words, Jesus,
now at the Father's right hand as our great High Priest, is working with all his strength to bring innumerable blessings to the
Church, "which is his body, the fullness of him who fills all in all"
(Eph 1:23).

Fullness for the Family

You can hardly believe that the church is God's fullness if you
look with the eyes of sight. It always looks weak and beggarly—
full of failure, not God. Yet because it's the family of the Father,
because it is inseparably the bride of Christ, because it is the
spiritual dwelling place of the Spirit, it is, in fact, "the fullness of
him who fills all in all" (Eph 1:23).

Because Jesus is head over all things for the Church, all of
the world's happenings, from the rise and fall of nations to the
smoking of volcanoes (Psa 144:5; 104:32), occur for the good of
the Church. When he appoints the boundaries and habitations of
the nations (Deut 32:8; Acts 17:26), it's for the good of the Church.
When he gives power to one of the enemies of the Church that
they might rule over it for a season, he's doing it to bless the
Church. Every fiber of Christ's being is towards us and for us.
His every thought, intention, and affection is to bless us, to love
us, to fill us, to inhabit us, to pour himself into us. There is absolutely nothing outside of his sovereign control, and he's been
set as head over all things for the express purpose of blessing
the Church.

The interjecting prayer of Paul's that we just looked at isn't an anomaly. If we go a little bit further into the book we'll find that he's been so caught up in the wonder of the truth he's trying to explain that he has tried to pray two or three times, but he hasn't quite got there because he keeps seeing more and more and more. Finally in chapter 3 he comes to prayer:

> For this reason I bow my knees before the Father, from whom every family in heaven and on earth is named, that according to the riches of his glory he may grant you to be strengthened with power through his Spirit in your inner being (Eph 3:14-16).

Why does he pray like this? Why ask that the Church be strengthened with power in the inner being? The Old Testament gives several accounts of the glory cloud of Yahweh coming (Exod 40:34-35; 1 Kgs 8:10-11; 2 Chr 5:13-14; Ezek 43:1-5). In Hebrew, the word for "glory" (*kavod*) comes from the word for "heavy" (*kaved*). Thus, glory is related to a certain weightiness, a heaviness under which the priests could no longer stand on their feet to minister. When we come into contact with the smallest glimpse of God's glory, just the smallest touch of his garment, we're rendered speechless.

There were numerous reports of great distress under the weighty hand of God in the great Hebridian revival of 1949 (Western Scotland)—hours of unbroken silence and stillness after the preaching of the Word. Duncan Campbell, one of the revival preachers, noted that a feature of the revival was the overwhelming sense of the presence of God: "His sacred presence was everywhere."[1] And it's for just such episodes that Paul prays for our strengthening with power through God's Spirit in the inner being. He prays so that we can bear the weight of glory that God has revealed to us.

> So that Christ may dwell in your hearts through faith—that you, being rooted and grounded in love, may have strength to comprehend with all the saints what

is the breadth and length and height and depth, and to know the love of Christ that surpasses knowledge (Eph 3:17–19a).

Who is Christ, who is the Father's Son, who is his Glory, which is brought to us by the Spirit in the inner being? How are we to see this? How can we know something that surpasses knowledge? On a simply human level, most of us have known the joy of companionship, whether with close platonic friends or in a marriage relationship. It's clear that we could spend all of our lives living and relating and never come to the end of that other person. In the living, dynamic movement of such fellowship, there's something at work that is beyond our ability to grasp or contain. It fills and gives life and expands our hearts one for another. This is just a "teaspoon-full" of what God has brought us in Christ.

"To know the love of Christ that surpasses knowledge"—this is the goal of Paul's prayer and his description of what God has done. "To know the love of Christ that surpasses knowledge, *that* you may be filled with all the fullness of God" (3:19)—this is where that goal is headed. To know experientially the fullness of God, to know the blessings which he has for us, is wholly wrapped up in our coming to see ever clearer the love the Father has for us in the Son.

God blesses us according to the riches of his glory. He doesn't give us just something *out of* the storehouse of his riches; he gives *according* to his riches. We think he gives like we do. We think if we are good, he might give us something we want. We think he might show us a bit of affection, or have some mercy on us when we are in need. But what God is able to do, and is doing, is far more abundant "than all that we ask or think" (Eph 3:20). God holds nothing back. He has given us all of himself in Christ Jesus. That's why Jesus used the generosity of a poor Jerusalem widow (Mark 12; Luke 21) to demonstrate what God's kingdom is like: She didn't give a tenth of her income, or even half, she gave all she had; there was nothing left. This is what God has done in Christ; he's given according to his riches.

His purpose to bless us in Christ is far greater than anything we could ever imagine. The nature of that blessing in Christ is far richer than anything we could ever hope for. But his riches are ours only as the eyes of our hearts are enlightened and our spirits strengthened in faith. They're ours only as we begin to comprehend the incomprehensible love of God for us. Then, and only then, do we begin to be filled with the fullness of God.

Struggling to Receive

Part of our struggle to receive the gift of God is this: All our lives we've been taught you don't get something for nothing, and what you earn is in accordance with how hard you work. But outside of faith in Christ's work, all our good works are essentially against God because they're an attempt to make a way for ourselves bypassing the cross. The grace of God can't be owned, bought, or earned. It's free and it's never going to end, because we never get to the end of *God*.

Too often in our Christian lives we run to the seaside with a thimble and run back to our houses exclaiming, "Look! Look what I've got." Then we spend the next two generations recalling what happened when we collected that thimble full of blessing. Putting the thimble on the shelf, it becomes a symbol of false worship as we idolize its first filling. And yet all along the rolling waves of the ocean are ever present crashing upon our very doorstep. The ocean—constant, rolling, breaking on the shore of our lives in grace, mercy, love, peace, joy, goodness, faithfulness, gentleness—is there for us because that's what the Father is in himself.

Christ comes to us not with closed fists and crossed arms. No, his hands and arms are flung wide open revealing his own open heart. The Father has given him to us saying, "Now you're one with him. He's come and embraced you as your bridegroom. You and he are one together in me. Do you not see, this is my very heart towards you?"

The Apostle Peter puts it slightly differently, but no less poignantly. "May grace and peace be multiplied to you in the knowledge of God and of Jesus our Lord" (2 Pet 1:2). Peter speaks in terms of multiplication, not addition. God's blessing has an exponential character. "His divine power has granted to us all things that pertain to life and godliness, through the knowledge of him who called us to his own glory and excellence, by which he has granted to us his precious and very great promises, so that through them you may become partakers of the divine nature," continues Peter (2 Pet 1:3–4a).

"That ... you may become partakers of the divine nature." Now, that's a bold statement! We wouldn't make that statement, but Peter did. Certainly there's a need, therefore, to be careful in the manner in which we think about it. It doesn't mean that we somehow become divine or become God. As someone once quipped, "He's 'da-vine,' we're the branches." We never become God. But in terms of fullness of his character, all the fullness of his grace, love, and mercy, all the fullness of the fruit of his Spirit, in all of these we become full partakers of the divine nature. That's the goal to which his promises are directed.

A Banquet of Unity

Jesus is not ashamed of those he calls his brothers and sisters, but rather he stands with them, saying, "Here am I and the children whom God has given Me" (Heb 2:13b NKJV; cf. Isa 8:18). This was always the Father's plan. In saying this, Jesus in effect is saying to the Father: "Look at what you've done. Look at the redemption you've won. Look at this family. Aren't they magnificent?!"

Every member of that family will be conformed to the image of Jesus Christ. We're one in him, inseparably bound to him. He has redeemed us from all of our transgressions, all of the brokenness of our lives. Everything that has been a ruinous waste he's now made a fruitful garden. Hence Jesus Christ is the new Eden; he's the place in which we dwell. Jesus Christ is the new temple; he is the place in which we receive fully the Father's glory finding that we can't stand under its wonderful weight. Jesus Christ is the new creation; everything we have we have in him.

The Scriptures give us a picture of the community in Christ whenever it alludes to a great banquet (e.g., Luke 14, 15; Psa 23; Isa 25:6). There the Father is in the midst of a great multitude providing a banquet for this family who participate in his joy. But this banquet isn't just any old feast; it's the culmination of fellowship on every level. It is a banquet of unity. The entire family of God in Christ Jesus, conformed to his image, his character, sings the same song that he sings, loves the Father with the same love with which he loves the Father, and is loved by the Father in the same way that he's loved.

We need to see God as Father; we need to see him as he is for us, how he sees us in his Son and Spirit, even now. Unless we start with this endpoint, we get a picture of God beginning with a good intention; human beings mucking it all up; and God coming up with an ingeniously clever rescue plan to get everything back on track, and then thinking, "What am I now going to do with them? Well, I've sent Jesus. Perhaps he'll be a good model and they'll learn to follow his example." But this entire storyline ends only in bondage to the law—even when it's the law of discipleship. Do you get that? It ends in bondage to law! Martin Luther argued that gospel understanding of Christ is primarily as gift, and not as example. He wrote:

> But I will not let this Christ be presented to me as exemplar except at a time of rejoicing, when I am out of reach of temptations (when I can hardly attain a thousandth part of his example), so that I may have a mirror in which to contemplate how much I am still lacking, lest I become smug. But in the time of tribulation I will not listen to or accept Christ except as a gift.[2]

Jesus didn't come to give us a good example, or to offer us assistance. He came to save us!

God's plan and purpose have always been that there would be a great multitude of sons and daughters conformed to the image of the Son. Angelic wickedness, human sin, the cross, the resurrection, the day of Pentecost, the final resurrection, are all part and parcel of God's plan to conform us to the image of his Son. We've trouble, however, comprehending that the sovereignty of God can be stretched so far. God doesn't take a *laissez-faire* approach to sin and wickedness. While this is evident, the "good news" is that our choices are never greater than God's purposes. Even the Apostle Paul knew the pain of acting in a way he didn't want to, yet he was confident that God would bring to completion the good work he'd begun in him (Phil 1:6), and in Christ he'd be sustained as guiltless to the end (1 Cor 1:8).

Eden was never finally what we were made for. We were made to be redeemed persons filled with the fullness of the Father through his Son, the lamb who was slain from before the foundation of the world (Rev 5:12). Simplistically stated, God never said, "Oops!" God's not playing "catch-up" after our sin and failure. Rather, we're in the business of catching up to what he's already purposed.

Expanded Vision

All of Paul's talk about the fullness of God, being filled unto the fullness of God, and receiving all of the blessing of the fullness of God draws out the skeptics in us, for it doesn't seem to fit our experience. We think, "Right. It all sounds a bit overly mystical and optimistic. And even if it just might be true, it's something that belongs to those special saints." *But this is what God has for every member of his Church.* He has destined everyone of us to be filled to that fullness. Yet still we play the cynic; "Well, maybe it will happen at the resurrection on the last day." Yes, but it starts now! It's what God has for us *even now*. Otherwise Paul would not pray for the enlightening of the eyes of your hearts "that you may know what is the hope to which [God the Father] has called you" (Eph 1:18).

In the parable of the Prodigal Son, the father says to the elder brother, "Son, you are always with me, and all that is mine is yours" (Luke 15:31). This truth is echoed by the Apostle Paul when he writes, "So let no one boast in men. For all things are yours, whether Paul or Apollos or Cephas or the world or life or death or the present or the future—all are yours, and you are Christ's, and Christ is God's" (1 Cor 3:21–23). God wants to turn us away from the thimbles we've carried into the sanctuaries of our hearts and enshrined there and instead turn us to the great ocean of his endless love that's breaking upon our doorstep, saying, "Look this way. Look this way. Because this is who I am, and this is where you really are in Christ."

It comes down to this: How expansive is our vision of the Father's plan? How expansive are our hearts? The Father loves to do for us "far more abundantly than all that we ask or think" (Eph 3:20a) because he's love and because he's our Father, and because he's already provided it all in Christ Jesus.

Why are we still focused on the thimble? Isn't there an ocean? What we call times of revival—whether they cover communities, cities, countries, or the small corner of the world which is our heart—are simply times in which our eyes are opened to see what is already there. The whole world is yours in Christ; God the Father is yours in Christ. Without the assurance of the love of God the Father, mediated to us by the Spirit in the person of his Son, we fear life and are terrified of death. If our hearts aren't enlightened to the gift of grace that God freely lavishes upon us, we'll be consumed with needing to "make a way for ourselves" and "twist God's arm" by our incessant good works to manipulate some small amount of blessing from him. But the Father's love is unstoppable, unquenchable, and abundantly greater than we could ever ask or hope for. It's poured out upon us now. May the eyes of your heart be enlightened to see where you really are in Jesus, to see that in him the whole fullness of the Father is yours.

CHAPTER 3

The Father's Plan

We often encounter a view of God—indeed, plaguing our own hearts—in which God is essentially against us; that he's only a hair's breadth away from crushing us, with the least provocation. To put it differently, we function as though we deeply believe that God's disposition is first and foremost anti-us and that we must do something to bend his heart towards us, to make him pro-us. This mode of thought, and the actions that flow from it, are completely contrary to the Christian faith. In fact, this is where Christianity separates itself from every other religion. The God of Christianity is for you and me; he is "pro-me." His "pro-*me*-ity" is the way he is; it's not something which he can or has to be cajoled into being.

What is the Christian life? The Christian life is constantly receiving, constantly hearing again that God is for me in Jesus Christ—this is the gospel. Jesus Christ is the "yes" of God's "pro-meity." And this means that the Christian life constantly involves the simple reflexive response of, "Amen, that's the way that it is!"

This response richly pleases God, for it gives all glory to his grace and keeps none for self. In sum, *the Christian life is continually receiving and responding to the gospel.*

The gospel places our salvation, welfare, blessing, dignity, identity, destiny, and the fruitfulness that God has promised us as his sons and daughters in a new creation, wholly outside of us. It occurs entirely *in God*, and it occurs in God *for me*. This "promeity" isn't based on what we each have done, are doing, or will do. God was, in fact, pro-me even when we were anti-him, when we hated him and in sin and rebellion preferred to be his enemy (Rom 5:6-10; Eph 2:1-10). It's this "promeity" of God—anchored in Jesus, outside of me—that is the principle of the Reformation. It's what Martin Luther discovered afresh. He came to understand that God's righteousness was also in God's being for him, and for his part, he was to live by faith in this very fact. When the reality of this divine "promeity" broke through into Luther's life it utterly changed him. He wrote:

> I greatly longed to understand Paul's epistle to the Romans, nothing stood in the way but that one expression "the righteousness of God," because I took it to mean that righteousness whereby God is righteous and acts righteously in punishing the unrighteous ... Night and day I pondered until ... I grasped the truth that the righteousness of God is that righteousness whereby, through grace and sheer mercy, he justifies us by faith. Thereupon I felt myself to be reborn and to have gone through the open doors into paradise. The whole of Scripture took on a new meaning, and whereas before "the righteousness of God" had filled me with hate, now it became to me inexpressibly sweet in greater love. This passage of Paul became to me a gateway into heaven.[1]

The sweetness that Luther experienced in his own heart for God was wholly anchored in God's loving-faithfulness extended to him, a love promised in the fulfillment of the new covenant (see Jer 31:31–34). In this new covenant, the Father fulfilled every promise he ever purposed. In this chapter, we want to explore the depths of his plan and purpose set before the foundation of the world (1 Pet 1:20), that we might come to take hold of the truth of his "promeity."

All Promises Are "Yes!" in Jesus

In Matthew 1:1, "Jesus Christ, the son of David, the son of Abraham" appears like a header introducing the subsequent genealogy. The genealogy is divided into three lots of 14 generations (cf. Matt 1:17), with Abraham and David serving as the first two major marker points (the third being the deportation to Babylon). The point of this "header verse" is to proclaim that all the promises given to Abraham, and subsequently to David as the offspring of Abraham, now fall, by line of inheritance and virtue of his incarnation, on Jesus Christ.

The great promise of Genesis 3:15 is passed to Abraham and reiterated to David; David's kingship in Israel would represent God's kingship over the nations. "Ask of me, and I will make the nations your heritage, and the ends of the earth your possession" (Psa 2:8); in 2 Samuel, when David wants to build a house for the Lord, God instead says, "No, David, 'the Lord will make you a house' " (7:11). David had in mind a physical temple. God, however, had in mind a house of a very different sense: a dynasty. "You will have earthly sons come from you," God says in effect, "but one will have an everlasting dominion, whose kingdom will never be shaken. The promises you receive in your enthronement will actually be inherited by your son—the farthest and future Son." And David can't believe his ears. He receives this gift of mercy and grace and wonders, "Is this your 'normal way' God? Is this your revelation for the nations, that you would come to me with a blessing that would touch the world? Is this the way you normally are?" And God's resounding answer, fulfilled in David's greater Son, is "Yes!" (see Matt 12:42; Mark 12:35–37).

And so the promise to Abraham is transmitted through Isaac, Jacob, and Joseph all the way down to David: that rest would come, that offspring would come, and that the nations would be blessed. By the time we get to David it's crystal clear that the promised blessing is going to flow out from his throne. All the promises that God has made from Genesis 3:15—"I will put enmity between you and the woman, and between your offspring and her offspring; he shall bruise your head, and you shall bruise his heel"—through the covenants with Noah, Abraham, Moses, David, and everything ever promised through the prophets concerning restoration and renewal, is going to be fulfilled in the anticipated offspring of Eve and of Abraham, the royal son of David, enthroned forever—the Messiah.

The history of God's Old Testament people showed that these promises were never fulfilled in any of their earthly rulers. The prophets looked and longed for the time of their fulfillment (1 Pet 1:10-11), and through them God made great promises to his people. He kept reiterating the covenant promises to the prophets and through them to Israel and to the nations. Even the prophets' pronouncements about God's necessary judgments stand in the context of his overarching commitment to his covenant.

Messianic expectation was high at the time of Jesus' earthly ministry. Many looked and longed for the Messiah's appearing (e.g., Luke 2:25-30), but nearly everyone misunderstood what he would be like. No one expected him to accomplish his work through the suffering of the cross. Jesus' disciples didn't understand this until after his resurrection. "Are you the Christ?" Israel wondered, but Jesus didn't fit. Yet the New Testament answer is, "Yes, indeed, Jesus is the Messiah ... but not in the way you expected him to be." It's as though Jesus says, "I am the Christ, yet I'm not going to be Christ in the way you want. For you want a Christ who establishes an earthly kingdom by power, a kingdom of political and military might. No, that's not who I am. Rather, I'm the sort of Christ who comes—as I always have—*for* the nations, not to exclude them. I'm the sort of Christ who comes with the heart of my Father, pro-sinners. I come for the ones whom you'd slaughter, for those you'd bring to your own judgment and crush beneath your chariots. This isn't the sort of Christ I am, because this isn't the sort of Father who has sent me."

Throughout Matthew's Gospel two themes continually emerge: (1) that Jesus is the fulfillment of all the Old Testament promises—note the recurring purpose statement, this was written so that it might be fulfilled (e.g., Matt 21:4; cf. John 19:24); and (2) that the great Davidic king would rule over the nations with justice and mercy, blessing them through the compassion and loving-kindness of God. Hence Jesus, being Abraham's offspring and of David's line, comes *through* Israel but not solely *for* Israel.

Throughout Matthew's Gospel we witness the nations coming in: wise men coming from the east (Matt 2:1); a Roman centurion blessing the Lord and receiving his blessing (8:5-13); the disciples being told to expect persecution that will result in their witnessing to the Gentiles (10:17-18); the healing of a Canaanite woman's daughter (15:22). As Jesus walked the roads of Israel, he was enacting the fulfillment of the Abrahamic promise. Though the Davidic king of Israel, he was already bringing God's blessing to the nations, extending his reign over them through his mercy. This reaches its climax at his death, where Jesus is portrayed as the completely unexpected king—robed in scarlet, a crown not of gold but of thorns upon his head, and a reed, a mock scepter, in his hand (27:28-29). How close to the truth they were. His reed scepter under a crown of thorns is a pretty good symbol of what his reign is really like—humble. And yet it was used as an instrument to mock: "He is the King of Israel; let him come down now from the cross, and we will believe in him" (27:42b).

But—precisely because he was the King of Israel come to bless the nations—coming down from the cross was the very thing he would never do. For his blessing of the nations was wholly bound up with what was happening on the cross; his blood shed was the inauguration of the new covenant (26:28; 1 Cor 11:25). In this covenant, the promises declared through the patriarchs and prophets—that there would come a time when a new covenant would be formed in which the forgiveness of sins would be complete and every heart cleansed (Joel 2:28-32)—finds its fulfillment. In this covenant, "no longer shall each one teach his neighbor and each his brother, saying, 'Know the Lord,' for they shall all know me, from the least of them to the greatest, declares the Lord. For I will forgive their iniquity, and I will remember their sin no more" (Jer 31:34). In this covenant, everything God ever promised his Old Testament people would be fulfilled.

Matthew 1:1 shows that the early church, encapsulated by the gospel, saw Jesus as the Messiah, that all of God's promises were fulfilled in him. His incarnation, death, resurrection, and ascension are the unexpected means by which they have been fulfilled. His reappearing at the end of this age will open his fulfillment of the great promises to sight—but now we live by faith. Regarding this fulfillment Paul writes:

> For all the promises of God find their Yes in him. That is why it is through him that we utter our Amen to God for his glory (2 Cor 1:20).

Paul is pointing out two intimately connected points. The first is that Jesus Christ is the embodiment and fulfillment of all the promises of God. A promise of a resting place for his people, a promise of redemption and deliverance from oppressors, a promise of his very own personal presence, a promise of new creation, of every nation belonging to God. Every promise that God has ever made has been fulfilled in Jesus Christ—he's God's "Yes!" to every promise. The second thing, flowing from the first, is that when we hear God's "yes" to us, a response of ratifying agreement, *Amen!* ("It is so!"), resounds within our hearts.

The Promise of Life

If we trace the history of God's dealing with humanity from the Old Testament onwards, we ought to naturally end up in a doxology something like this:

> Your promise Lord is all I have,
> My only hiding place.
> The Rock of refuge where I fly,
> To seek and find your face.[2]

As we've just seen, from the beginning God has been a God of promise. His heart as the Father-Creator is full of blessing. From that point onwards, we see the continual purpose of God is to bring blessing, even in the face of human sin and evil. Our mistake is we don't know what we need. Too readily we decide for ourselves or others what "blessing" should look like, and too readily assume that suffering and adversity are signs of God's curse. But, if we've been blessed by our heavenly Father "with every spiritual blessing in the heavenly places in Christ" (Eph 1:3), we ought not assume that adversity is necessarily a sign of God's disfavor. In fact, God graciously brings and allows much that seems to be against us with the purpose of hemming us in more closely to the full dimensions of his blessing (cf. Joel 2:25).

The words of blessing God speaks, and his actions in bringing them to us, are received by faith. When God speaks, he speaks real and true blessing, but from the point of view of our receiving it at a time yet to come, it is "promise." The blessing is certain because it is pronounced by God, yet we do not necessarily receive the fulfillment of it in our present experience. And so we are carried onto the path of faith and there we walk, anticipating the full revelation of that which is already ours now (1 Cor 1:7). We live by promise; "we walk by faith, not by sight" (2 Cor 5:7).

Paul makes much of this. For him *promise* is primary, couched in terms of God's gracious covenant. As a typical example, God blesses Abraham with wonderful covenant promises in his first encounter with him. Notice that God was pro-Abraham, even while Abraham was still anti-God—indeed, an idolater from Ur of the Chaldees (Josh 24:1-3). God's being *for* Abraham was not based on Abraham's righteousness in keeping God's commands. God's promise to Abraham is but the expression in human history of the prior promise of God to Adam.

The first, greatest, and perhaps the most comprehensive promise is found in Genesis 3:15. God announces that one would come—the offspring of the woman—to bruise the head of the serpent and be bruised in the process. In other words, this one would nullify and remove all satanic opposition towards God, and the old serpent, the devil, would be trodden under foot. This cosmic victory would win humanity's freedom from condemnation and from the fear constantly inculcated by the serpent in the human heart through accusation (well founded and accurate!) related to our sin and failure. We're not innocent bystanders, but exist in a state of enmity towards God. Our sin is real, deep and ineradicable by any human means. The serpent's accusations intensify our guilt and shame, consolidating us in fear of God's judgment. We hate God and wish he were dead. When his Son comes, we kill him, because in killing him, we strike at the one who sent him (Matt 21:33–39). Yet God's purpose is that in this hate-filled and inexcusable action, he would bring us into his promised blessing.

This great promise of Genesis 3:15 is sometimes called the *protoevangelium*, which simply means that it's the first proclamation of the good news to sinners, and is the outworking in human history of the eternal "promeity" of God towards his beloved children. Even as they turn their faces from him, hide beneath fig leaves, and suffer exile from the garden, God's face remains set towards them. He makes provision for them, covering them with animal skins and showing the sacrificial process needed to atone for and cover sin (Gen 3:21). Sin and the satanic evil that stimulated it shall not be the last word governing creation. A divine promise shall reign: *The woman's Son shall destroy the devil's schemes.*

From this promise onward the question is: Through whose line will this offspring come? And we see distinctions occurring. There's a distinction between Cain and Abel: Cain is not of the offspring of faith. According to John, he "was of the evil one" (1 John 3:12). When Cain murdered Abel, God gave another son, Seth. It's through Seth's line—not Cain's—that the people of faith came, those who "began to call upon the name of the Lord" (Gen 4:26), eventually leading down through Noah to Abraham (Gen 5:28; 11:26).

From Abraham's line come Isaac and Jacob, and from Jacob, the tribes of Israel. Throughout the genealogy the question is in the foreground: Who's the offspring? Is Isaac the one? In a sense, yes, and there's a distinction between him and Ishmael; Isaac is the son given by promise and beheld in faith (Gen 21:12-13). Yet Isaac isn't the final awaited offspring. Isaac begets Esau and Jacob, parental competition and favoritism ensue, and another distinction is made by God: "I have loved Jacob but Esau I have hated" (Mal 1:2-3). Ah, so it's Jacob who is the promised offspring? Yes, but not definitively. Jacob has twelve sons and another distinction is made, this time for Judah and his line (see Matt 1:1-17). Time and again we find the apparently unassuming genealogies reeking with rivalry and reprobation—yet God preserves the line of the offspring of faith. His promise to Abraham reflects that which was made to Adam: that through his descendant all the nations of the earth would be blessed. When God comes to us, even in the midst of judgment, he comes to bless.

Sometimes we really struggle with this. We struggle with the thought that his love is so strong and his desire to bless is so intense. Our deeply ingrained work ethic causes us to view everything God does in utilitarian terms. If God does something, it must be because he wants us to do something in return. To think he might just want us to enjoy it is a bit of a stretch for us—it strikes us as unspiritual. And yet such an attitude actually smacks of self-righteousness. It displays a heart that is wholly oriented to works of the law as a means to climb out of personal guilt and to protect oneself from shame. This is blindness to sin and deafness to the promise. It's not seeing God as Father.

In reality, God might not want us to do anything with a blessing except to enjoy it, to love it, to be stunned by the beauty of it, to be overwhelmed by the grace of it, to share the blessing with others. It brings joy to a parent to see their child enjoying something they'd given him or her. And so similarly the Father's joy is bound up with the joy of his children, as he brings us into the fullness of his own fatherly joy. When we enjoy the blessings of our heavenly Father, we find our greatest pleasure in him and with him. Yes, there are works for us to participate in, but these are ones that our Father has planned before the foundation of the world for us to walk in (Eph 2:10). They're works of love and mercy, works of justice and joy. They're works given to us in Christ, not ones that we offer to him by way of payment in order to win his favor.

When Abraham received the promise of blessing, it was for him and his children to enjoy. Abraham and Sarah enjoyed the blessing, laughing because they couldn't believe that it could be so good. And they called their son Isaac, which means "laughter." The Lord's promises to Abraham were a lifeline in a life of wandering, learning at every turn, "The Lord will provide" (Gen 22:14). Despite all of his faults and failures, Abraham enjoyed life and found his pleasure in God's continual presence.

Promise Precedes Law

In delivering Israel from slavery in Egypt, God remembered his promises to Abraham. To this redeemed people he gave the gift of the law through Moses. They didn't earn their redemption by keeping the law. The law was a gift that followed redemption.

Abraham himself, many centuries before, while he was still a pagan worshiper of strange gods in Ur, received God's promises. God came to him, turning him from his idols, and sending him out from his father's house. With God's promises of blessing came a command to circumcise all the males born as his descendants (or adopted into his household) as a sign of the covenant. Abraham wasn't blessed, however, because he circumcised his children.

He was blessed before he ever received such a command. Circumcision was a *sign* that he'd been blessed by God's grace, not a *reason* for God to bless him. There is a critical order here: first promise, then revelation of the law.

This is exactly Paul's theme in Galatians 3-4: The law wasn't given to nullify the promise, but to serve it; that is, to show us the promise is all we have to stand on. For by no means could anyone attain righteousness by works of the law. By keeping the law, says Paul, comes knowledge of sin. The law brings wrath, it stirs up sin, it reveals our unrighteousness, it shows us what's in the very depths of our hearts. The more we use the law, the greater the sin in our hearts is stirred up. The question that Paul is after in Galatians 3 is: What's the purpose of the law? The answer, ultimately, is that the law shows us that being right with God has always occurred by *promise*, never by obedience to the law. How misguided we are, thinking we're going to earn God's favor by attempting to keep the law, which itself condemns us in order to drive us to the promise of grace!

It's in light of all of this that Paul tells us the law didn't come to cancel out promise, but so that promise may be *truly and purely* promise (Gal 3:17-22; Rom 7:7-8). If anything could show that an individual or a nation couldn't achieve righteousness on the basis of law, the history of Israel is it. They had it all: the covenants, the law, the temple, the prophets. But even with such a rich heritage they didn't achieve righteousness, because righteousness isn't gained on the basis of ritual and moral law-keeping. The law just instructs as to what sin is, it convicts us, but *it cannot grant us the ability to keep it from the heart*. Attempted law-keeping doesn't make us righteous—if anything it makes us self-righteous—and this is why righteousness is granted from above on the basis of God's promise, not works. "A person is not justified by works of the law but through faith in Jesus Christ, so we also have believed in Christ Jesus, in order to be justified by faith in Christ and not by works of the law, because by works of the law no one will be justified" (Gal 2:16).

Blessing Bound to the Coming Son

What we've said thus far comes to this: The promised blessing to the nations is bound up with the Son's sacrificial death, through which he opens up the new covenant promises to them and removes the curse of the broken law. George Smeaton states the cosmic dimension of this truth well:

> Sin was the ground of Satan's dominion, the sphere of his power, and the secret of his strength; and no sooner was the guilt lying on us extinguished, than his throne was undermined, as Jesus Himself said (John 12:31). When the guilt of sin was abolished, Satan's dominion over God's people was ended; for the ground of his authority was the law which had been violated, and the guilt which had been incurred.[3]

In the account of the exodus, God in essence shouted to Pharaoh with signs, wonders, and judgements, "Let my people go!" (Exod 8:21a). But when Jesus achieves our exodus he does it surprisingly quietly. If our release could be accomplished by some exercise of metaphysical power, so to speak, then there wouldn't have been a need for him to take on human nature in the incarnation and experience the horrifying death of crucifixion. But since "sin was the ground of Satan's dominion, the sphere of his power, and the secret of his strength," Satan could only be neutralized through sin's removal. If "the ruler of this world" (John 14:30) were to be cast out, his power base (of our sin and its attendant guilt) would need to be breached. Only in the cross could this be done.

Satan came at Christ with everything he had. Have you ever had to survive even one night of piercing accusation under Satan's hand? Have you tried to make it through the night with a conscience carrying the burden of the broken law? It just rips you to pieces. Our experience of such can garner only an infinitesimally small appreciation of what Christ must have endured as he was made sin for us (2 Cor 5:21). No doubt as he was made sin for us, bearing our guilt, he was subject to the whole host of darkness and demonic accusations hammering into him, but he stayed on that cross and endured it all until it was finished. In other words, *for us* he descended into the deepest abyss of suffering, even hell itself, and there—emptying himself by taking on our plight of utter alienation from God—in solidarity with us, triumphed.

No sooner was the guilt lying on us extinguished, than Satan's throne was undermined. Jesus released us from the rulers and authorities (Eph 6:12) "by canceling the record of debt that stood against us with its legal demands" (Col 2:14). He nailed our record to the cross and thereby "disarmed the rulers and authorities and put them to open shame, by triumphing over them in him" (Col 2:15). It means that all of our sins are forgiven. *It means a new covenant has come!* It means the Father has fulfilled his promise: "For I will forgive their iniquity, and I will remember their sin no more" (Jer 31:34); "I will remove the heart of stone from their flesh and give them a heart of flesh" (Ezek 11:19); "I will sprinkle clean water on you, and you shall be clean from all your uncleannesses" (Ezek 36:25).

The power that Satan has over you and me, the power he has over the church, is to tell us there is still sin that has not been dealt with, that there are still things that have to be atoned for, that there is still something yet to be worked out. He fills us with fear because fear involves punishment. We fear to come to the Father because we are not fully and completely convinced that he has entirely dealt with everything. But he has dealt with our past, present, and future trespasses "through the offering of the body of Jesus Christ *once for all*" (Heb 10:10). And if that certificate of debt which is full of decrees against and hostile to us, which never says a good thing about us, if that is gone, what power does Satan have? The answer is, none. We know this victory only by faith, and live in a world in which it's constantly contested.

A friend in Scotland once told me a story about his father who worked in the mines as a fireman (that is, one who set the dynamite fuses). One day there was a mishap with one of the machines. His father could see that another man's life was in danger and he put his hand out to hit the emergency stop button, but his hand got caught in a cog and it chopped off the top of one of his fingers. For years afterwards, particularly when he was down in the mines, he would find himself clutching where the finger used to be because it was full of pain—even though there was no finger there. This is known as phantom pain. And it's what Satan inflicts upon us.

Everything is finished on the cross, the certificate of debt has been removed, all sin has been forgiven. But the accuser keeps coming at us, telling us that it's still there. He keeps it ever present before us—and it feels so real, as though it were still there—such that we end up nursing our wounds. But they're phantom pains. The accuser troubles us with what has already been dealt with. That's why he doesn't want this gospel to go out to the nations—he doesn't want God's people to go free.

Yet through the proclamation of the gospel God is bringing about a new exodus, saying to Satan, as to Pharaoh of old, "Let my people go!" And Satan, the spiritual pharaoh, has his heels dug in, screaming, "No!"

The Lord replies: "My Son has come in whom the promises are Yes and Amen (2 Cor 1:20); there is nothing left to be done, for he has accomplished everything. I have raised him from the dead as a vindication that it's finished, and he's seated at my right hand as proof that he's Lord of all. The Holy Spirit has been poured out so that this gospel would be preached, and all the nations would receive the Spirit of my Son and turn to me saying, 'Abba! Father!' (Gal 4:6), rather than cowering in fear."

All of this has occurred "so that in Christ Jesus the blessing of Abraham might come to the Gentiles, so that we might receive the promised Spirit through faith" (Gal 3:14). For where the Spirit of the Lord is, there is liberty; where the Spirit of the Lord is, there is no longer a reminder of sins; where the Spirit of the Lord is, there is just a testimony to Christ that looks away from self and to the Lamb. And where the Spirit is present, there is a deep cry for the Father. Sons and daughters are brought home through the proclamation of Christ. When we come to know this truth of our sonship, instead of living in fear our hearts cry out, "Amen!" That "amen" is worship.

CHAPTER 4

The Lord in Our Midst

Sing aloud, O daughter of Zion;
    shout, O Israel!
Rejoice and exult with all your heart,
    O daughter of Jerusalem!
The Lord has taken away the judgments against you;
    he has cleared away your enemies.
The King of Israel, the Lord, is in your midst;
    you shall never again fear evil.
On that day it shall be said to Jerusalem:
"Fear not, O Zion;
    let not your hands grow weak.
The Lord your God is in your midst,
    a mighty one who will save;
he will rejoice over you with gladness;
    he will quiet you by his love;
he will exult over you with loud singing.

I will gather those of you who mourn for the festival,
    so that you will no longer suffer reproach.
Behold, at that time I will deal
    with all your oppressors.
And I will save the lame
    and gather the outcast,
and I will change their shame into praise
    and renown in all the earth.
At that time I will bring you in,
    at the time when I gather you together;
for I will make you renowned and praised
    among all the peoples of the earth,
when I restore your fortunes
    before your eyes," says the Lord (Zeph 3:14–20).

Zephaniah wrote these words to a people facing impending ruin. Judah's captivity was certain, secured by her persistent rebellion against God. But rather than receiving contempt from God or an aloof "I told you so!," God sent his prophets to warn of coming destruction and promise redemption. While never delighting in calamity he was bringing, such judgments proved the Lord was near (Zeph 1:7).

Instead of abandoning his people, *God enters into their midst to save.* The failure of Judah and Israel wasn't the last word. Through Zephaniah, Jeremiah, Ezekiel, Isaiah, and others, God repeatedly said, "There's a word beyond that of your failure; there's a word beyond judgment; there's a word beyond exile; there's a word beyond fruitlessness." And this word is God's word of *promise*, the promise of a new covenant and of a coming messiah. In the words of Zephaniah, who lived during the reign of Josiah not long before the fall of the kingdom of Judah, this is expressed as the coming "day of the Lord" (e.g., 1:7, 8, 14). The day of the Lord is not just an ancient promise to Judah and Israel, it's also for us—today, in and through judgment, God comes to save his people from themselves.

God comes so sin won't have the last say. Such grace isn't the natural result of what happens when we're deserving of it—entitled grace isn't grace!—but grace comes because of who God is in himself, despite our unworthiness. He's the Father who doesn't abandon but seeks out his besieged children to remove our enemies and our shame, and bring us peace. He rejoices loudly over us; his song is the cause for our songs. Knowing such joy is the heart of this chapter.

Wonderful Promises for Woeful Days

Zephaniah's prophecy arrived at a desperate time when Judah was near the end of her independent existence. She was decaying inside, and powerful enemies were massing on her borders. Soon Babylon would invade and overrun. God warned, and Josiah listened.

Josiah was a good king in a history riddled with wicked kings. Indeed, with the exception of David, he was the pick of the litter (see 2 Kgs 22–23; 2 Chr 34–35). The difference between a good and wicked king wasn't brilliance in governing or extraordinary personal righteousness. King Omri, for example, was a great administrator and builder, but received a negative review: "Omri did what was evil in the sight of the Lord, and did more evil than all who were before him" (1 Kgs 16:25). David, on the other hand, wasn't spotless; he did many shameful things. Yet he was called a man after God's own heart (1 Sam 13:14) because he recognized that the Lord was the savior and refuge for his people and entrusted himself and the people to him. That's the difference: The Old Testament delineates good kings by the fact that they led God's people in worship of the Lord and away from those things which ultimately ended in self-trust. In other words, they led them away from idolatry, which, in any form it takes, is fundamental trust in the work of our own hands, rather than God's.

Josiah recognized the nation's problems weren't political or economic, but spiritual. Clever alliances or more legislation wasn't going to fix it. *The problem was the nation's heart, its corrupt worship.* By his time, the temple in Jerusalem—which should have been the place where people were taught to trust God—had become a repository for false gods and superstition. The people had turned to mediums and diviners for guidance. They erected shrines to other gods on high places throughout the land, even burning their children as offerings. Our idols always demand more and more of us, until we've offered up our very lives.

In addition, the Holy Scriptures had been lost, Passover hadn't been celebrated for years, and legitimate prophets were ignored or persecuted while the warm words of false prophets were honored. Far from the Lord, the people grew—just as we do—self-centered, insensitive, and resentful. The nation was saturated with greed and corruption; men and women preyed on each other rather than served one another in love. It was utter spiritual and moral decay.

So Josiah sought reform. His reform was good and thorough, and the Scriptures were rediscovered after a hundred years, but it was too late. The prophets could see that the nation's heart was settled in its rejection of God; other kings would not follow in his steps; and God's corrective discipline was already in motion. The hand of the Babylonians had been strengthened, their army would lay siege to the city, the walls would be breached, the temple torn down, and thousands would be exiled—dismal news.

"But take heart!," the prophets urged: Judgment wasn't to be the last word, the end of a grim story. Rather, God is beautifully at work dealing with his people for their good and his glory. Reality is full of light and hope, even when all we can see is the outright opposite, because God's mercy comes in the midst of and even *through* judgment. The nation's failure, David's failure—Peter's failure, *our* failure—isn't the last word. True hope lies not in the ability to extricate ourselves from the darkness of our failure, but in God's own willingness to send and be our unfailing light.

Zephaniah had to prepare the people for God's coming by planting within their hearts a longing for the day of the Lord—ultimately for them a day of salvation, not of destruction. His promise of a "day" wasn't a threat of unending wrath against God's children, even for their consistent and irremediable failure. It was a promise of his entrance into the very midst of the besieged city to revive, to restore, to heal, to bring low the high places, and to make whole. Looking forward to this day of the Lord, Zephaniah calls for deep joy rather than sorrow:

> Sing aloud, O daughter of Zion;
> > shout, O Israel!
> Rejoice and exult with all your heart,
> > O daughter of Jerusalem! (Zeph 3:14).

This is the way our Father speaks: a wonderful word to a woeful situation. Yes, they may be words of rebuke and discipline, but they always lead to hope. As such they are different from those of Satan. He accuses, leaving us feeling condemned, hopeless, frightened, and angry. We fight to justify ourselves and make excuses. But the voice of God—*even in rebuke*—comes with hope and blessing. It leaves us feeling as if we have been honored with a great gift; the Lord disciplines the *children he loves* (Heb 12:6). The Lord's discipline is full of promise, not threat, setting us free to love and be loved.

Perhaps you are reading this book from within a deep and dark valley, a difficult and painful place in which you're prone to stumble and lose sight of the one who's leading you through it. Know that Satan adds his voice to the noise, tempting towards despair. He seeks to paint God in ugly colors and cause us to fear and question his goodness and purposes: "Why me, why this? Is this all you have for me, Lord?" Or you may have a heavy burden for the church; not just your particular fellowship or denomination, but the Church, as the universal people of God. You deeply feel the all-too-apparent lack of grace and love. Well, the psalmists felt it, too. In places like Psalm 80, where Israel is likened to a vineyard with its walls broken down and the vineyard laid waste, there's a cry for the restoration of God's people. It may seem like everything is shriveling, that fruitfulness has departed, that God is no longer sought after, that hope has withered. And upon your heart sits the question: "Is this all there is ... have you abandoned us, God?"

Do not judge God's ways by what your eyes see and your ears hear. For the Father is present to save, and his reply to both yearning questions is identical: "'Rejoice and exult with all your heart, O daughter of Jerusalem!' (Zeph 3:14). *For your failure and my judgments are not my last words.* There is a day—wait for it."

From Zephaniah's point of view the day was yet to come. And often in our dark valleys we are too depressed and tired to wait in hope for some distant day. Yet in the reality of Christ's finished work on the cross and his resurrection, "the day" has already begun to dawn, and we have great cause to shout for joy. The relief and revival you seek hasn't been overlooked by our heavenly Father; he's *for you* in mercy and love. The cries and questions we address to God are as much a sign of his presence as the flooding rains, for through them he's drawing us to himself. Our today is as precious to him as our tomorrow.

The Besieged City

The picture of God's sinful and suffering people we find in Zephaniah is that of a city surrounded by impending calamity, with no way out. When a city was besieged in the ancient world, it was a brutal and protracted ordeal. It could last for years as the populace was broken and starved into submission. For those inside, the encamped army was a constant testimony to their inescapable shame. Deliverance for a besieged city or a besieged heart has to come from outside.

Our world is fearful of the future. If you listen to the underlying tone of the global media there's a deep rhythm pounding out, "Disaster! Disaster! Disaster!" Financial crises, political gridlock, ecological catastrophes—the Lord touches the mountains and they smoke! (so Psa 104:32)—and everything is thrown into chaos. Uncertainty and cynicism are the hallmarks of our world. Nations retreat into protectionist policies. We retreat into self-defensive ways of relating. Despite the relative material security of our generation in the developed world, we suspect that we feel more insecure than ever. Personal insecurities trouble us as much as national and global crises.

The deep beat of impending disaster, however, isn't confined to media, politics, or psychology; it echoes in the church. The rise of secularism, the possibility of persecution on our doorstep, the passing of prejudicial legislation—in sum, the world, the flesh, and the devil—surround us in order to stir up strife and to accuse. Even in our Christian lives the drums thump with the voice of our adversary "who accuses [us] day and night before our God" (Rev 12:10). How often we hear his persistent voice louder than that of our faithful Father! Does the accuser ever say a pleasant word, ever bring a word that leads to quiet waters and green pastures? No, he threatens, undermines, and then abandons us to the fear of disaster. He appeals to the law for our condemnation— and there is plenty of ammunition there! He never utters a good word to or about us. Or if he does, it is only to magnify our pride and self-reliance. His testimony *always* leads us away from the grace of our Father to fear of his presence.

The work of the devil among the people of God is like an unruly dog who has intruded on a sheep pen. The dog runs and barks until it gets the sheep in a frenzy, pinned up in a corner against the fence. He singles out one sheep at a time from the rest of the flock, leading it to doubt that it ever belonged to the flock in the first place. *All the sheep can hear is the voice of the dog, and all they can feel is fear.* They certainly can't hear the shepherd—and will they be trapped forever? Perhaps the shepherd isn't strong enough or doesn't care enough to silence the intruder?

Are you familiar with the reality of this situation in your own life? When we are besieged like this our own heart is of no help. Sometimes when we're under attack, when the world, the flesh, and the devil all seem to be colliding on top of us in what Martin Luther referred to as the great *Anfechtungen* (the times of overwhelming spiritual trial, suffering, and tribulation in which it feels that God might judge and condemn you at any moment)—at those moments we can look to the Scriptures for help, and even they might seem like nothing more than a dead letter. In the *Anfechtungen* we certainly can't hear the Shepherd.

But then, *from outside* comes rescue—someone sends help, a word proclaiming peace. Zephaniah's word to Israel and Judah in light of that day was such a word, but it was also something much more:

> The Lord has taken away the judgments against you;
>   he has cleared away your enemies.
> The King of Israel, the Lord, is in your midst;
>   you shall never again fear evil (Zeph 3:15).

Israel and Judah discovered that the judgments coming against them, from the Assyrians in the north then the Babylonians in the south, were to be of such magnitude that they wouldn't be able to penetrate enemy lines or find help to avert the disaster. God certainly judges sin, including our sin. But again, he comes to his sinful people in love, to cleanse, to discipline. He comes to us from outside, and judges and saves within. Though it hadn't happened yet, Zephaniah speaks as though this deliverance from judgment was already accomplished. He speaks in the past tense about the future, because the Lord's deliverance is so sure, the word of his coming so real, and the covenant he would establish beyond the broken covenant so certain, God's future for us *cannot not happen*. About a hundred years later—still waiting!—Zechariah echoes Zephaniah's prophecy with the following words:

> Rejoice greatly, O daughter of Zion!
>   Shout aloud, O daughter of Jerusalem!
> Behold, your king is coming to you;
>   righteous and having salvation is he,
> humble and mounted on a donkey,
>   on a colt, the foal of a donkey (Zech 9:9).

In the history of Israel, this prophecy and others like it repeatedly led the people to ask when, where, and how these promises would be fulfilled. They grew up under the prophets, in a time of expectation of a coming deliverance from God—a coming Deliverer. So when the New Testament opens, what do we find but magnificent descriptions of the coming of the Son of God.

In this light, the significance of the incarnation—the Word becoming flesh—is that *the Lord comes and reveals himself in our midst to save*. He doesn't stay outside the city, outside the human experience, and from there wage war on the enemy. He enters into the thick of where the enemy resides—that is, he enters into the human mind and heart, and human rebellion. We are our own enemy, for we carry within us our very temptability.[1] It is our proneness to sin that Satan exploits so very well and which is the ground of his accusations.

Besieged on Our Behalf

Jesus' entrance into the sinful human fray, however, doesn't seem like such a victorious rescue. For he comes as a fetus in the womb; he comes through the normal developments of childhood (Luke 2:52). As such he's hidden, incognito, not recognizable by sight. And yet, he's no less Emmanuel, God with us, God in our midst recognized by faith.

At Jesus' baptism, as all the people come in repentance to the Jordan river to be baptized by John, Jesus responds to John's protest against baptizing *the one man who needs no repentance*: "Let it be so now, for thus it is fitting for us to fulfill all righteousness" (Matt 3:15). In saying this, Jesus intimately identifies himself with those sinners coming for baptism. "It is fitting for *us* to be baptized, John. These people and I are one. They are my people, and I have come for them." Jesus is one with us. He is in our midst, in our flesh, and in our blood, "born of a woman, born under the law to redeem those under law, that we might receive the full rights of sons" (Gal 4:4-5).

Likewise, the Lord's coming into the midst of besieged Jerusalem is fulfilled as Jesus comes up from Galilee. In his final journey, he comes as a victorious warrior, "riding on a donkey, the colt of a donkey" (Matt 21:5; fulfilling Zech 9:9) to end the captivity of the people of God. But in all this Jesus remains incognito except to faith. Usually conquering kings rode on war horses, but Jesus comes in humility, showing himself to be the servant-king of peace. He comes in a weakness totally inappropriate for any earthly conqueror. In him, the promises of God are "yes" (2 Cor 1:20), but not in the way we expect. But his "weakness" is perfectly fitting for the Lamb of God, the incarnate Son in our midst, *the Lord who is willingly conquered in order to gain his people's victory.*

Jesus comes to deliver by riding into the very heart of Jerusalem, surrounded by physical as well as spiritual enemies. But riding into the center of Jerusalem isn't the deepest heart of his journey, because inside Jerusalem is waiting condemnation to death on a cross outside the city. His journey went from heaven, to the womb of Mary, into the wilderness, through his public ministry, into the heart of Jerusalem, and right down into the depths of human darkness and divine judgment. The Apostle Paul seeks to describe this profound mystery when he says, "For our sake he made him to be sin who knew no sin, so that in him we might become the righteousness of God" (2 Cor 5:21). Whereas the crowds all along were looking for glory, honor, and power on their terms, Jesus' true power lay in his humility. He came as a servant to die on a cross.

In light of the cross, we can't mistake Jesus' journey for simple solidarity, the action of a noble man empathetic with the plight of others because he's liable to the same fate. Rather, in his holiness he voluntarily endured *the abyss of who we are* in all our wickedness. The besieged city of Jerusalem is but a picture in time and history of us all. Jesus went into the pit of what comes out of the sinful human heart: idolatry, enmity, strife, jealousy, anger, rivalries, dissensions, divisions (Gal 5:20).

"The King of Israel, the Lord, *is in your midst!*" cries Zephaniah (3:15). In the midst of what? In the midst of our sin; in the midst of our failure; in the midst of our filth. The Lord is in the midst of human destruction. He is in the midst of our hatred of God and one another. He is in the midst of our idolatry. *The Lord is in the midst of his enemies.* The weight of sin pressed in on him; the evil one with all of the forces of darkness gathered around him full of accusations and threats:

> Many bulls encompass me;
>> strong bulls of Bashan surround me;
> they open wide their mouths at me,
>> like a ravening and roaring lion.
> For dogs encompass me;
>> a company of evildoers encircles me;
> they have pierced my hands and feet—
> I can count all my bones—
> they stare and gloat over me;
> they divide my garments among them,
>> and for my clothing they cast lots (Psa 22:12–13, 16–18).

Little wonder, then, that Jesus cried out with a loud voice, "My God, My God, why have you forsaken me?" (Psa 22:1; cf. Matt 27:46; Mark 15:34; Luke 24:44). Becoming our sin and shame, he entered the wasteland of human wickedness and experienced God's wrath against it. And by going into the fullness of those depths *for us*, he redeemed the whole of who we are *to God*.

Do you see, then, why Zephaniah cries out with news not of despair but of joy, "Rejoice and exult with all your heart, O daughter of Jerusalem!" (3:14). Rejoice over this? Why? Because *in your very midst* "the Lord has taken away the judgments against you; he has cleared away your enemies" (Zeph 3:15). Oh, but we so often don't see it. We don't realize it until by grace the Spirit of the Lord himself comes again into our midst and opens our eyes. We are blinded by two foes: the accuser and our own hard hearts, refusing to see "the glory of God in the face of Jesus Christ" (2 Cor 4:6). Unbelievers don't realize they're surrounded by enemies—sin, death, the devil, and the curse of the law—and far too often the believing church doesn't sense the danger or rejoice in the news of salvation, either.

Is it a struggle for you to be a Christian? Are your days filled with recommitments to try harder, to reform your life so God will look upon you with favor? Then you remain a slave to sin and under the curse of the law. Yet it's likely not in the manner you may think. You remain a slave to sin not because you continue to struggle with it, but because of *the false impression that deeper dedication and effort to obey the law will set you free*. It will not, and it cannot. Only the gospel frees you. What is needed is simply to take God at his word—to entrust yourself to God by the grace of his Spirit—and you will be changed, at the deepest levels of mind and heart, by the love of the Father displayed supremely through Jesus' work on your behalf.

Receiving the Victorious News

A besieged city is cut off from hope and given over to despair. Relief for such a city doesn't come through the recitation of what it *ought* to have done, or the preparations it *should* have made. It's in need of a word of rescue from outside. And this is just what Zephaniah proclaims in the passage we've been looking at in this chapter. But as we noticed earlier, that word concerning the day of the Lord wasn't just for Judah and Israel. It's also for us. It's a word proclaiming the coming of Christ and his saving work in our midst: The battle is over; the victory is won; God is with us.

How does the besieged city or heart learn the victorious news? The Word of deliverance itself has to enter it. God enters into our lives in Jesus; as he rode into Jerusalem in humility, he rides into our hearts with gentleness and grace. He calls us to know his love for us, and from within that experience to simply trust him in every aspect of our lives—to lay down our arms and know the joy of his peace.

So that we don't let the point escape us, it's important to emphasize that commandments, commitments, and conduct (i.e., works of the law) cannot avert sin's siege. The law brings no exclamation of delight, because "the law is not of faith" (Gal 3:12). It issues commands, but doesn't give motivation or ability to fulfill them. The battlefield is not outside us; it is inside us, in our very hearts, so striving to do better completely misses the heart issue. The law's function has always been to reveal our sin and to condemn us (Rom 3:20), that we might be driven to Christ where alone we hear good news of great joy (Luke 2:10). There is a champion who is for us, among us. He has come into the very midst of our battlefield, and there all the haunting of the powers of hell raged against him; there he knew curses instead of blessings; there he proclaimed, *"It is finished!"* (John 19:30); and there God's weakness was victorious over the strongest foes (1 Cor 1:25). He is victorious, and so *our* victory comes, even in and through sin and suffering, when by the grace of his Spirit we place our confidence only in *his* victory—do you get that? This is a message that we all need to hear repeatedly, for we quickly forget in the chaos caused by the barking dogs of our consciences and the accuser.

Faith comes by hearing, not just once, but throughout our entire Christian life. When your sufferings are most intense, when you lose the ability to speak the gospel to yourself, you're not abandoned by God or his people. From some quarter someone comes uttering the Word, setting before you the promise of hope and life and the message of an undying love that won't let you fall. There is life in that message, *from the outside in.* Hold on to it. In it you are justified, protected, and whole. Dietrich Bonhoeffer put it well when he wrote:

> God has willed that we should seek and find the living Word in the witness of a brother, in the mouth of a man. Therefore, the Christian needs another Christian who speaks God's Word to him. He needs him again and again when he becomes uncertain and discouraged, for by himself he cannot help himself without belying the truth. He needs his brother man as a bearer and proclaimer of the divine word of salvation. He needs his

brother solely because of Jesus Christ. The Christ in his own heart is weaker than the Christ in the word of his brother; his own heart is uncertain as his brother's is sure. And that clarifies the goal of all Christian community: they are to meet one another as bringers of the message of salvation.[2]

Since the judgments against us, each and all, have been removed in the cross of Christ, then God has taken away the ground on which our enemies have been encamped. The siege is lifted; that which fills with fear and threatens disaster is gone. We might not see things changing as quickly as we desire, but all has been accomplished. We can be quieted by the Father's love, for his Son is in our midst—we can trust his promises.

CHAPTER 5

The Father's Cross

The very early church contended with an unorthodox teaching, one that periodically reemerges in different forms, called patripassianism. It's the idea that God the Father died on the cross. This teaching was rightly rejected; nevertheless, it was trying to guard against another problem that should also be taken seriously: that on the cross God the Son stands with and for us *over against* God the Father. This isn't the case at all. Rather, as the Son willingly undertook our salvation, so the Father *initiated* salvation: He sent the Son (1 John 4:14), made him to be sin (2 Cor 5:21), and judged him in our place. Jesus went to the cross, not because the Father's against us, but because he's for us.

The incarnate Son didn't protect us from the Father, but in counting our trespasses against him the Father disclosed his own purpose for us. The Swiss theologian, Karl Barth, put it this way:

> What took place is that the Son of God fulfilled the righteous judgment on us human beings by himself taking our place as a human being, and in our place undergoing

the judgement under which we had passed. ... Because
God willed to execute his judgment on us in his Son, it
all took place in his person, as his accusation and condemnation and destruction. He judged, and it was the
judge who was judged, who allowed himself to be judged.
... Why did God become a human being? So that God as a
human being might do and accomplish and achieve and
complete all this for us wrongdoers, in order that in this
way there might be brought about by him our reconciliation with him, and our conversion to him.[1]

The cross is the point at which God exposed our delusions—
our wanting to be judge—and announces his judgment on such
sin. At the same time, he simultaneously took that same judgment upon himself in Christ. In other words, Jesus doesn't *block*
the Father's wrath due us, but *bears* it for us in order to *bring* the
Father's love. In this specific sense the cross isn't only Christ's,
it's also the Father's. It's the event in which his heart for us is
most thoroughly seen: "For God so loved the world, that he gave
his only Son. ... For God did not send his Son into the world to
condemn the world, but in order that the world might be saved
through him" (John 3:16, 17). Jesus never sought to appease a distant and angry Father.

Seeing the Father in the Cross

Sometimes we make the mistake of projecting everything wrong
with our earthly fathers—or mothers, for that matter—onto God.
What's wrong with many of our parents, however, is they honest-
ly don't know how to love us. Yet our heavenly Father *is* love, and
the cross is the act of his love in the Son, revealed to our hearts by
the Holy Spirit. This truth we desperately need to see, and grow
deeper in seeing. The cross is the quintessential unveiling of the
Father's heart. Apart from it we can't know the Father in himself.
We, the authors, think the following two passages state succinct-
ly the unified message of the New Testament:

All this is from God, who through Christ reconciled us to himself and gave us the ministry of reconciliation; that is, in Christ God was reconciling the world to himself, not counting their trespasses against them, and entrusting to us the message of reconciliation (2 Cor 5:18–19).

In this the love of God was made manifest among us, that God sent his only Son into the world, so that we might live through him. In this is love, not that we have loved God but that he loved us and sent his Son to be the propitiation for our sins (1 John 4:9–10).

No other place besides the cross enables us to know the Father so fully, because no other place enables us to know the forgiveness of sins. The great new covenant promise—"No longer shall each one teach his neighbor and each his brother, saying, 'Know the Lord,' for they shall all know me, from the least of them to the greatest, declares the Lord"—is only possible because of this complete removal of our sin: "For I will forgive their iniquity, and I will remember their sin no more" (Jer 31:34). "In this is love, not that we have loved God but that he loved us and sent his Son to be the propitiation for our sins" (1 John 4:10).

The Father initiated the work of the cross, but the Godhead is at work in accomplishing it. The Latin phrase *opera ad extra indivisa Trinitas sunt* summarizes this, meaning, "The outward works of the Trinity are indivisible." In other words, Father, Son, and Holy Spirit are each full-hearted participants in all God's dealings with creation. The Father was in his Son reconciling the world *to himself*, and the Spirit enabled the Son to offer himself as the pleasing sacrifice. The cross is the work of the Godhead, flowing from the Father's initiating, sending, delivering-up, judging, redeeming, raising, and settling a new creation, all of which is his activity of reconciling the world to himself. And by this the Father ensures that all his people will be conformed to the image of *his* Son, in whom we see *his* face (John 14:9–10). Reconciliation through the Son, in the Spirit, moves us to the Father that God "may be all in all" (1 Cor 15:28).

Some very useful terms are used in Scripture to help us understand how God the Father in particular accomplished this reconciliation. In fact, understanding the scope of the whole Old Testament is required to comprehend the work of Christ on the cross—in wonderful themes such as the temple, priesthood, substitution, laying on of hands, imputation of sin, shedding of blood, holy of holies, mercy seat, exodus, justification, sanctification, and on and on.

But please don't think that any of these themes, as important as they are, take us by themselves to the heart of the cross. They might describe something of what God has accomplished there, something of the fruit of his work, but they don't unveil the heart of the matter. As we interact with these as mere concepts, bundling and taping down all our theories, we are in danger of domesticating the cross in such a way that God doesn't have room to move. We can be so self-righteous in our knowledge, or so rigid in the explication of our systematic theology, that we might be a million miles from *really embracing* what it meant for God to be in Christ reconciling the world to himself. P. T. Forsyth begins to get at this when he writes:

> [Christ's] revelation was action more than instruction. He revealed by redeeming. The thing He did was not simply to make us aware of God's disposition in an impressive way. It was not to *declare* forgiveness. It was certainly not to *explain* forgiveness. And it was not even to *bestow* forgiveness. It was to *effect* forgiveness, to set up the relation of forgiveness both in God and man. ... The great mass of Christ's work was like a stable iceberg. It was hidden. It was His dealing with God, not man. The great thing was done with God. It was independent of our knowledge of it. The greatest thing ever done in the world was done out of sight. The most ever

done for us was done behind our backs. Only it was we who had turned our backs. Doing this *for us* was the first condition of doing anything *with* us.[2]

Because the cross is first and foremost a work of *God himself for himself*—the Son of God becoming a man, accomplishing his Father's eternal counsels in the Spirit, bringing everlasting glory to himself and grace to us—it is a kind of "singularity." That is, at the cross all our normal ways of thinking and speaking disappear into infinity. From one point of view, everything that happened shouldn't have: How could the God who is love do this to his Son? But from another point of view, how could the God who is love *not* do it—he who has loved us in Christ before the foundation of the world (Eph 1:4-6)? And so in our reasonings we come to the black hole, the impenetrable darkness behind the veil.

Second Corinthians speaks of a great exchange: "For our sake he made him to be sin who knew no sin, so that in him we might become the righteousness of God" (5:21). This verse and others like it get us thinking in terms of marriage, so that all that belongs to Christ the bridegroom becomes ours, and all that's ours becomes his. Theologians call this imputation. It's right and helpful, but it's not our focus in this chapter. Rather, we need to see that in bringing about this great exchange the Father mercifully gave everything for us. This moves us even closer to the heart of God.

Anomalous Destruction

The very last word of the Old Testament is the Hebrew word *khārem* ("curse, utter destruction"):

> Behold, I will send you Elijah the prophet before the great and awesome day of the Lord comes. And he will turn the hearts of fathers to their children and the hearts of children to their fathers, lest I come and strike the land with a decree of *utter destruction* (Mal 4:5-6).

Throughout the Old Testament *khārem* was that which was given over to destruction, things such as the worship of idols and the false sacrifices of the high places. In considering passages that speak about such destruction, a picture emerges of the "great and awesome day of the Lord" as God's judgment on all that doesn't belong to him, all that is eternally *khārem*.

Judgment day is coming, Malachi says, but one is coming before that day who will turn the hearts of the children to the fathers, "lest I come and strike the land" (4:6). Here is an implication that unless God comes in mercy, the course of the human heart, family, and society will be ever downward. Unless he does something to "turn the hearts of fathers to their children and the hearts of children to their fathers," the only option is *khārem*. Yet unmitigated destruction, while the last word, is not the final word. The promise of a prophetic minister of grace comes as well. Jesus identifies this "Elijah" as John the Baptist (Mark 9:11–13), sent "first to restore all things" (Mark 9:12), to cry in the wilderness: "Prepare the way of the Lord; make straight in the desert a highway for our God" (Isa 40:3; cf. Mark 1:3). But what was he to prepare the way for? John was sent to prepare for the day of the Lord's manifestation in and against Jesus, as he became *khārem*, given to destruction.

Our point isn't that Jesus was there by and for himself, but that he was there *in* flesh and blood, *for* flesh and blood. As one who knew no sin, Jesus took sin upon himself and offered himself for it, that God might condemn it in the flesh (2 Cor 5:21). In Jesus Christ, in the fullness of time, the curse was executed so that through him it would be removed from us: "There is therefore now no condemnation for those who are in Christ Jesus" (Rom 8:1). And it all occurred behind our backs, while we were turned in rejection of God (Rom 5:8). The only place humanity stood face to face with him was at the cross, our hands holding the nails and spears. There we exclaimed, "At last, we've killed God!" But how can you kill love? For as Charles Spurgeon so vividly said:

His love that chose us did not shrink back from the awful payment which our debt rendered necessary: it was stronger than death, and mightier than the grave. Many waters could not quench it; many floods could not drown it; nor will it cease to exert its blessed influence over us until it shall bring us home to the mansions above; and not even then, for Christ's love is everlasting.[3]

The cross is therefore an utter anomaly, a complete reversal of everything expected. Jesus, the anticipated righteous branch under whose shade his people were to find shelter, the deliverer from the line of David, "a shoot from the stump of Jesse" (Isa 11:1; cf. Jer 23:5; 33:15; Zech 3:8–10; 6:12), was cut off and consumed by fire in a single day. On the cross the *one* righteous man was considered a criminal and crucified by so many unrighteous men. The truth was taken for a lie. The loving shepherd of the sheep killed. The bridegroom separated from his bride. The most-beloved Son, disinherited. The only-begotten Son, forsaken.

What was it for the Holy Spirit to be the Spirit of judgment and division, rather than the Spirit of unity between the Father and Son, to bring curses without measure to rest upon Christ's head rather than the fullness of blessing? What was it for the just judge to become the judged? For the only one who lived by mercy to receive none? For the peace of the world to be treated as an object of warfare? He became for us a besieged fortress whose walls were smashed, a vineyard trampled by beasts, a pillaged city in smoking ruin. The light of the world went into the darkest place imaginable, a place concealed from the Father's countenance, separated from the peace of his presence, a stranger to the covenant promises.

What pride when we dare think that we have this sorted out and filed away! Our theories can attempt to describe it, but they can't *touch* it. We've absolutely no grounds for theological snobbery. For at the point where the Son was in the place of judgment, if ever the Father loved him and was pleased with him, it was then. If ever the Father's loving kindness was being revealed, it was then. If ever the Father's heart was full of love for us, it was then. Human reason simply can't grasp the depth of the wonder or even the irony in all this. God explodes all our expectations and concepts in fulfillment of his promise: "I will remove the iniquity of this land in a single day. In that day, declares the Lord of hosts, every one of you will invite his neighbor to come under his vine and under his fig tree" (Zech 3:9–10). While we cannot fathom God's grace, let us not fail to worship him for it.

Abraham had to take Isaac, his most beloved son through whom God was to fulfill his promises, up Mount Moriah to offer him as a sacrifice. And yet God spared Isaac, staying Abraham's hand from plunging a knife into the heart of his son. But God didn't protect himself from the same dilemma. He couldn't send a ram as a substitute, as he did for Isaac, because his Son *is* the lamb.

The Father's Heart

We dare not think that because this sacrifice was predestined before the foundations of the world (1 Pet 1:19–20), it came easily to our Father's heart or smoothly to his hand. As the event of the cross reached its climax in time and space, we are granted a window into the depths of God's heart for us. We can't look at the cross and think that it cost the Son everything, while the Father experienced nothing. God is not pushed or pulled in subjection to the created order or overmastered by emotions. But he certainly doesn't fail to feel with utter fullness and perfection all that accords with his loving and gracious character. *The cross is Mount Moriah without restraint.* We can't hear the words of Hosea, which look upon generations of Israel's unfaithfulness, and fail to discern the real heartache of the Father:

> Oh, how can I give you up, Israel?
>   How can I let you go?
> How can I destroy you like Admah
>   or demolish you like Zeboiim?

My heart is torn within me,
and my compassion overflows (Hos 11:8 NLT).

So what must it mean for the Father to consider his beloved Son, bearing humanity's sin in body and soul, and then abandon him to utter destruction? Again, we, the authors, don't think we can appeal to the reality of God's sovereignty, decrees, and predestinating purpose in order to suppose that God is aloof or unfeeling. God is not Stoic, and God's sovereignty and purposes are misunderstood if they are wrongly placed in contradiction to the richness and activity of God's thoughts, feelings, and desires. Indeed, we must recognize that in the cross-bearing of the Son, the Father also mysteriously yet truly entered into the most acute agony of that innocent-yet-cursed man who was God. But this is the beauty of it all: God himself has freely entered the darkness of human sin and suffering through the Son, out of sheer love, *and is wholly satisfied.*

We all have trouble overlooking each other's mistakes without conveying that "the least we could do" is really as much as we're willing to do. We take great care to make sure our magnanimity isn't forgotten, thinking no less of ourselves for being so "gracious." But this isn't forgiveness or generosity at all; it's a graceless way of dealing with the ungracious. Forsyth beautifully contrasts God's liberality with our stinginess:

> It would not be like the grace of God, it would be ungracious, if He came forgiving man and yet laying more stress on what it cost Him to do it than His joy, fullness, and freedom in doing it.[4]

Where do you stand? In disbelief, unforgiving because you don't accept forgiveness from God? In aloof complacence, because you've neatly filed away God and his ways in the comfort of your own preconceptions? Or in faith, trusting in the message of the Father's self-giving love? If the last, then by this faith you stand reconciled to him in Christ, called by the Spirit to rest in the accomplished work of God our Savior.

In the cross we see that the Father, too, has loved us freely and fully. And if by the Spirit you've caught a glimpse of the depths of God's unfathomable mercy, don't feel guilty for how much your redemption "cost God." The Father saves us out of his abounding sufficiency, not from any need or lack. His love is *wholly* free. And don't feel sorry for the Son because of his suffering. Rather, *look to him*, who "for the *joy* that was set before him endured the cross, despising the shame, and is seated at the right hand of the throne of God" (Heb 12:2). The Father's desire is that you would come into the knowledge of such unending love, and experience the joy of such perfect peace. "In this is love, not that we have loved God but that he loved us and sent his Son to be the propitiation for our sins" (1 John 4:10).

CHAPTER 6

Freed to Rest

In the opening chapter of Luke's gospel, the Holy Spirit gives John the Baptist's father, Zechariah, the following words:

> Blessed be the Lord God of Israel, for he has visited and redeemed his people and has raised up a horn of salvation for us in the house of his servant David, as he spoke by the mouth of his holy prophets from of old, that we should be saved from our enemies and from the hand of all who hate us; to show the mercy promised to our fathers and to remember his holy covenant, the oath that he swore to our father Abraham, to grant us that we, being delivered from the hand of our enemies, might serve him without fear, in holiness and righteousness before him all our days. And you, child, will be called the prophet of the Most High; for you will go before the Lord to prepare his ways, to give knowledge of salvation to his people in the forgiveness of their sins, because of the tender mercy of our God, whereby the sunrise

shall visit us from on high to give light to those who sit in darkness and in the shadow of death, to guide our feet into the way of peace (Luke 1:68–79).

John's ministry is announced here, but the song is mainly about the greater work God will do through the ministry of Jesus. John, as great as he will be, will only prepare the way for the Lord's own arrival.

And notice what Jesus said of himself, reading from Isaiah 61 in the synagogue to announce the beginning of his public ministry:

> The Spirit of the Lord is upon me, because he has anointed me to proclaim good news to the poor. He has sent me to proclaim liberty to the captives and recovering of sight to the blind, to set at liberty those who are oppressed, to proclaim the year of the Lord's favor (Luke 4:18–19).

Jesus came to set us free, to proclaim that *this* year, *this* day, this very moment is the time of deliverance, the jubilee, the fulfillment of his promise of freedom. This is what Zechariah's song and Jesus' reading declare so openly. Christ "gave himself for our sins to deliver us from the present evil age, according to the will of our God and Father" (Gal 1:4). This is the wonderful gospel. And as it impresses itself upon our lives, as we grow deeper in the realization of it, our response to all of life is radically changed. Knowing that the Father is for us in Jesus isn't a dead fact—*it's a life-giving reality*. It enables us to face whatever might come against us or whichever of our failures Satan might hold before us (John 4:14). Christ hasn't come to rehash our sin or expose our shame, but to deliver us and restore us to true sonship, a place where we stand upright in the peace of God that surpasses all understanding. Recalling this good news guards our hearts and minds, if we'll only strain to hear it (Phil 4:7).

In Jesus we see that God is present to set his people free from Satan's bondage—from "our enemies." He's bound the strong man and even now is plundering his house (Mark 3:27). Examining our release from captivity to sin and death, however, isn't our whole focus in this chapter, even while we devote much space to it. Rather, there is a deeper purpose in discussing it: *to see how this central and fundamental fact provides for the liberty of everlasting rest in God through Christ.* We, the authors, want you to catch a glimpse of what this facet of enjoying sonship looks like. Our desire is that you would come to experience the freedom and rest in God amid life's challenges, a perspective on life gained only through being a freed son or daughter of the Father.

A Disabling Spirit

In this light, let us consider Jesus' healing of a crippled woman on the Sabbath. Jesus' work here is nothing less than a picture of God's whole action in the history of the world. Here, too, the Lord is seen crushing the head of the serpent (Gen 3:15), setting his people free and relieving them from the burden of sin's curse.

> Now he was teaching in one of the synagogues on the Sabbath. And there was a woman who had had a disabling spirit for eighteen years. She was bent over and could not fully straighten herself. When Jesus saw her, he called her over and said to her, "Woman, you are freed from your disability." And he laid his hands on her, and immediately she was made straight, and she glorified God. But the ruler of the synagogue, indignant because Jesus had healed on the Sabbath, said to the people, "There are six days in which work ought to be done. Come on those days and be healed, and not on the Sabbath day." Then the Lord answered him, "You hypocrites! Does not each of you on the Sabbath untie his ox or his donkey from the manger and lead it away to water it? And ought not this woman, a daughter of Abraham whom Satan bound for eighteen years, be loosed from this bond on the Sabbath day?" As he said these things, all his adversaries were put to shame, and all the people

rejoiced at all the glorious things that were done by him
(Luke 13:10–17).

This "healing" is perhaps better expressed as "deliverance."
The woman was ill, but in this case her disability was caused by
an evil spirit. While we shouldn't adduce from one particular
case an assumption that all illness is cause by demonic oppres-
sion, neither should we ignore the Bible's testimony that sometimes suffering is caused by this. "For we do not wrestle against
flesh and blood, but against the rulers, against the authorities,
against the cosmic powers over this present darkness, against
the spiritual forces of evil in the heavenly places" (Eph 6:12).

For 18 years this dear woman had been afflicted by an evil spirit
which manifested itself in the crippling of her body. It's perhaps
easier to understand our attitudes and actions being the realm
where spiritual problems can exhibit themselves, but our physical bodies can display their effects, too. So Psalm 38:

> There is no soundness in my flesh
>> because of your indignation
>> there is no health in my bones
>>> because of my sin.
> For my iniquities have gone over my head;
>> like a heavy burden, they are too heavy for me.
>
> My wounds stink and fester
>> because of my foolishness,
> I am utterly bowed down and prostrate;
>> all the day I go about mourning.
> For my sides are filled with burning,
>> and there is no soundness in my flesh.
> I am feeble and crushed;
>> I groan because of the tumult of my heart (Psa 38:3–8).

Here David speaks of sin which had become, first, a spiritual
burden too heavy to bear. But we shouldn't relegate this to mere
metaphor. He speaks of physical sickness too: bodily pain, open

sores, perhaps fever or ulcers (his "sides filled with burning"). And he's in no doubt that his physical ailments are part of the burden of sin he's wrestling with in his heart. Coming to realize and own this, he pleads with the Lord that this burden might be lifted from his body as well as his soul.

David is bowed down and prostrate in mourning over his sin. But the woman in Luke is physically bent over and unable to release herself even to stand up straight. This woman was displaying in her *body* that she wasn't *spiritually* free. Sin's curse isn't just physical death; it's a spiritual death in which—not realizing the providential love and care of the Father—we war against him and each other. It's bondage to a life of continual strife and struggle, a life filled with anxiety, defensiveness, competition, and animosity. We don't know the precise roots of her affliction. But somehow or another a foothold was gained; something in her life was used against her and was too much for her to bear. She's in need of deliverance—a deliverance which heals both the spiritual and physical aspects of life, like God's deliverance of Israel from slavery in Egypt.

Pharaoh, after all, was the political ruler of Egypt as well as its spiritual ruler, a god on earth. So when we read of the event of Israel's exodus we shouldn't simply think of it as deliverance from the sting of Pharaoh's whip. Israel was ultimately delivered from the tyranny of the "gods of Egypt" (Exod 12:12). As Israel's toil and hardship went on, their anxiety and animosity grew. They lost their peace and rest; they questioned God's care; distrust festered in their bones—the hearts of God's people grew hard. So hard, that even after God's great deliverance from Egypt they still struggled to trust him as a faithful Father (Exod 16:2–3; 17:2–3; 32:1; Num 14:1–4).

Pharaoh, who neither knew nor recognized Moses's God, is a picture of the god of this age, who refuses to bow to our Lord Jesus Christ. The devil won't let God's people go free, seeking to "blind the minds of the unbelievers, to keep them from seeing the light of the gospel of the glory of Christ, who is the image of

God" (2 Cor 4:4). The exodus, as a picture of the Father's deliverance of his children in Jesus, flows into the Gospel narratives and the Epistles, so that in thinking on the work of Christ the idea is planted firmly in our minds that a new and greater exodus is occurring. Jesus is true Israel, the faithful Son (Matt 2:15). In him, a Passover lamb is sacrificed and a Pharaoh defeated. Jesus is the greater Moses who leads his flock to freedom, and feeds them with the bread of heaven, himself (John 6:51). And as Israel was delivered, this crippled woman is healed.

Healing on the Sabbath

The healing, however, took place on the Sabbath. God rested from his initial work of creation on the seventh day, and he invites his people to enter that rest, to know and enjoy him as Father. It's almost as if God created Adam and Eve on the sixth evening so that on the seventh morning they would figuratively "awake" to everlasting rest. The seventh day has no morning and evening formula because it never ends. God has created us to be at rest—not to be inactive or unproductive, but to be at peace, to live in the fullness of his blessing, our hearts filled to overflowing with his love.

But the Sabbath also has another dimension. In Deuteronomy 5:15, Moses speaks of the Sabbath as a remembrance of how Israel was enslaved in Egypt and how God heard their groaning and had mercy on them. They were to have rest on the Sabbath because they were once without it. That's why the writer to the Hebrews tells us that our Sabbath is secured in Jesus Christ, who is our everlasting rest (Heb 3:7–4:13). Isn't this what sonship is all about? It's resting in the fatherhood of God, free from fear, at peace in Christ amid the muddle of life. In the Sabbath, God's people are meant to enjoy a foretaste of that future rest.

And yet this dear woman in Luke has no rest from her suffering, and she receives none from those who were supposed to be able to help, the Pharisees and other religious leaders. This was not the only time they took offense at Jesus doing wonderful works of mercy on the Sabbath (see Matt 12:9–14; John 7:21–24; 9:13–16).

They didn't realize that what they needed most was not rest from certain actions, but rest with God from the heavy burden of a sinful heart.

Do You See This Woman?

When on another occasion Jesus visited Simon the Pharisee's house, a different woman with a different set of spiritual struggles came in with an alabaster flask of expensive perfume to anoint Jesus' feet. She came in seeking forgiveness, and her grief overcame her: "Standing behind him at his feet, weeping, she began to wet his feet with her tears and wiped them with the hair of her head and kissed his feet and anointed them with the ointment" (Luke 7:38). Uncomfortable with this disreputable woman in his house falling all over his guest, Simon commented under his breath: "If this man were a prophet, he would have known who and what sort of woman this is who is touching him, for she is a sinner" (Luke 7:39). In turn Jesus told Simon a parable and hit him with a simple question: "Do you see this woman?" (Luke 7:44). In other words, do you really see *her*? Or do you see a theological problem? Do you see an ethical dilemma? An opportunity to protect yourself from "contamination"? If any of these is all we see, then we don't see a real person in desperate need of the gospel. Too much of our lives is just like that. We don't see each other; we don't see others as people to whom Christ came to bring freedom and rest.

The same question to Simon must be asked of our dear woman in the synagogue on the Sabbath. Did anyone see her? Of course they saw her—doubled over in deformity, they couldn't miss her. And most people probably thought they saw her properly: "Oh, there's that woman, she's always been odd like that—bent and twisted. Probably getting what she deserves, I reckon." But there was only one who *really* saw her: "Jesus saw her, he called her over and said to her, 'Woman, you are freed from your disability'" (Luke 13:12). Not a single question about what she'd done to deserve this, no guilt or shame or disgust thrown at her. Just a declaration of the sheer gift of miraculous deliverance: "Woman, you are freed." Then Jesus "laid his hands on her, and immediately she was made straight, and she glorified God" (Luke 13:13). Notice the parallel with Israel's exodus:

> I am the Lord your God, who brought you out of the land of Egypt, that you should not be their slaves. And I have broken the bars of your yoke and made you walk erect (Lev 26:13).

> And [Jesus] laid his hands on her, and immediately she was made straight, and she glorified God (Luke 13:13).

How long since someone had touched this woman? How long since anyone had embraced her as a real person? How long since anyone had *seen* her and *loved* her nonetheless?

There's a deep irony here. The Pharisees patrolled the boundaries of the Sabbath, watching like hawks to see who was in bounds and who wasn't. They wanted to make sure people honored God on the Sabbath. Yet they were zealous that people understood the law and kept it only so God would bless them and others would admire their holiness. The irony is, no matter how zealous they were for the Sabbath, none of them ever would or could *heal this demon-troubled woman to the glory of God.*

Yet as soon as Jesus spoke to her and touched her, she realized that the Lord himself is for her, not against her. Receiving his affection she stood up straight and glorified God. Jesus did by grace in an instant what the Pharisaic spirit couldn't do in a hundred lifetimes: He released her from Satan's bondage and brought forth a wellspring of praise from her heart. Because he was to become the sin of the world, he alone could say, "Woman, you are freed." "Whatever the cause of your burden, whatever this demonic spirit is accusing you of, I've taken what is yours and given you what is mine. Stand upright! For my yoke is easy and my burden is light." When we are truly ready to entrust ourselves to the Lord this lightness becomes our joyful burden, too.

The irony of the Pharisees's impotence to heal is further pressed home when Jesus responds to their grumbling over the Sabbath laws:

> "You hypocrites! Does not each of you on the Sabbath untie his ox or his donkey from the manger and lead it away to water it? And ought not this woman, a daughter of Abraham whom Satan bound for eighteen years, be loosed from this bond on the Sabbath day?" (Luke 13:15–16).

The same verb, "loosed," is used in this passage for the untying of animals and the binding of the woman. The Pharisees have more compassion for their animals than for this suffering child of God. That's the Pharisaic spirit: sanctimonious self-righteous hypocrisy. But let's be honest with ourselves: That's you and me. If we take a good long look into our own hearts none of us can claim to be any better than the Pharisees. How do you see your neighbors, your spouse, your children, or even fellow Christians who don't fit your mold? Are they the outcasts, the unorthodox, the unethical? They might be, but Christ has come for them as he has for you, because he has come for *the ungodly* (Rom 5:6). He sees them and wants to touch and heal them, as he is healing you.

Freedom and Rest

Like the crippled woman, all the people Jesus met were real people with real spiritual troubles. But what happens for the one is also representative of the whole. In a sense, this woman is us, just as the woman at the well and the woman caught in adultery are. Our own spiritual disabilities are exposed by Peter in his denials and Saul in his self-righteous and hateful legalism. We see in Jesus' deliverance of the crippled woman a specific manifestation of the one great exodus, through which the Lord brings his people to their place of rest. He delivers us from bondage, breaking the power of the usurper-god Satan. Through the cross,

God himself achieves the rest he ordained for his children from the beginning.

The twisting of such great mercy which happened among the Pharisees shouldn't really catch us off guard, because we're all too familiar with it in the church today and in our own lives. What God gives by grace as a blessing, we turn into a means by which to earn his favor and lord it over others. It's the way the human heart is until grace comes—until God's free favor in Christ delivers us and this freedom is driven deep into our hearts by the Holy Spirit.

We, as the authors, don't know how you see yourself. Many see themselves as restless failures. They haven't lived up to the expectations of everyone around them, and even more so they're aware of failure before their most important audience, God. If you see yourself as a worn-out slave to expectations you're constantly failing to live up to, then you're not living in light of the reality of freedom and rest that belong to the Father's children. Do bondage to sin and an absence of peace characterize you? If so, as uncomfortable as it may be, ask yourself: Have I really grasped the gospel?

Even so, the truth of the gospel is that God knows all our failures; he sees all our spiritual disabilities; and in his grace and mercy he has delivered us from sin, self, and Satan. "As far as the east is from the west, so far does he remove our transgressions from us. As a father shows compassion to his children, so the Lord shows compassion to those who fear him" (Psa 103:12–13). This is what Jesus has accomplished for us and made known to us. He's disclosed the Father's loving heart, at peace with us and welcoming us as sons and daughters. This is our identity, no matter how we've failed to meet expectations, no matter what allegations the accuser whispers to the contrary. Let us trust God's Word rather than Satan's.

Do you believe Jesus sees you as you are and cares for you? He does. He sees your situation, your turmoil. He sees the weight of the law that doubles you over, the spirit of legalism that squeezes the life from you. He sees the accusations of the Devil that hammer in your ears telling you that you couldn't really belong to the people of God. He sees your very real sin and shame and failures. He also sees the anxiety, austere struggle, and animosity that can fill the hours of your days. He sees all this and says, "You are freed from your disability. All is done, all is finished. Your burden is gone, because I've borne every bit of it in *my* spirit and *my* body on the tree. Come to me, find deliverance and rest."

The Test of a True Christian

Freed and healed, yes! But what day-to-day difference does it make? What does standing up straight look like? We can assure you that Jesus' words of deliverance are much more than mere consolation. In a word, being set free in body and soul from sin and its accusations means *rest*. On one hand, it's rest from the struggle of having to earn God's favor and friendship. He came to us before we ever went looking for him (Rom 5:8). But on the other hand, it's rest from those strains and struggles of life stemming from our own sin and that of others.

The significance of the fulfillment of God's promise in Eden—that a son would come to crush the head of the serpent—is that our Father's goodness and faithfulness towards us has been proven true (cf. Luke 4:18; John 3:16; Gal 4:4-6). No matter where we are or what we're going through, it's crucial to remember God's character and his heart for us. He sees us, just as he saw the dear crippled woman and distressed Israel. In fact, lingering on this in the midst of trial is really the only thing able to alter our response to them. Other things may momentarily distract our unbelieving hearts, but our Father's faithfulness to remove our sin and provide for our daily needs (Matt 6:25-26) is the only thing that effects deep and lasting trust in our hearts. This is resting in God and this is the true test of a Christian.

The test of a veritable faith isn't orthodox theology, as vital as this is. One can give intellectual assent to the best teachings, yet be spiritually dead. And while it's also true that "faith apart from works is dead" (Jas 2:26), moral conduct isn't foolproof evidence of Christian faith, either. Many live ethical lives benefiting others while denying the faith, so like the Pharisees they remain plagued by anxiety, defensiveness, competition, performance, and animosity. Similarly, a great crisis or climactic experience can shake us to the core and turn us in an entirely different direction. Certainly no one is born a Christian—we must be born again, and so religious experience is an essential part of knowing that the Spirit of God is dealing with us and has given us new life. But other religions also claim "mountaintop" experiences. So experience isn't foolproof evidence, either.

Rather, the true test of a Christian is his or her reaction to life. That is, a Christian's response to what happens to him or her flows from a heart that's experienced God's deliverance, rests in him by faith, and for this reason exhibits a new perspective and a new ethic. How do you respond when everything around you is falling apart, when the chair is swept out from beneath you, when you're face to face with calamity and you've come to the end of yourself? Can you join the Apostle Paul in saying that your troubles are light?

> We do not lose heart. ... For this light momentary affliction is preparing for us an eternal weight of glory beyond all comparison, as we look not to the things that are seen but to the things that are unseen. For the things that are seen are transient, but the things that are unseen are eternal (2 Cor 4:16–18).

Though we struggle daily with sin and doubt, Christians trust that God sees us and that he has freed us. Through our light and momentary grief our Father is bringing us into his everlasting glory. Our suffering is light because Christ bore it for us, and so we lean on him. This is the difference that Jesus' healing and deliverance makes, for such a perspective wraps up doctrine, morality, and experience in utter reliance upon the Father's goodness and faithfulness.

After losing his life's fortune in real estate investments in the Great Chicago Fire of 1871, and then losing his four daughters when the steamship ferrying them to England for a family vacation sunk in the mid-Atlantic two years later, Horatio Spafford echoed Paul's convictions in the words of a hymn:

> When peace, like a river, attendeth my way,
> When sorrows like sea billows roll;
> Whatever my lot, Thou hast taught me to say,
> It is well, it is well with my soul.
>
> Though Satan should buffet, though trials should come,
> Let this blest assurance control:
> That Christ hath regarded my helpless estate,
> And hath shed His own blood for my soul.

And there it is—a modern Job clinging to his God because he knows there's nowhere else to turn. Spafford didn't say "It is well" because he was cold or heartless—nothing is easier than apathy. He was convinced "it is well" because he knew his heavenly Father.

You can't speak like that unless the Father's victory achieved in the cross of Christ has loosed you from Satan's shackles. Only lingering on and transfixing ourselves to the proclamation of the cross ushers in a peace that overwhelms our hearts and alters our actions. Here, then, is faith; here is embracing God as Father. Here we are free to rest.

Whatever you've come into this book with, whatever is doubling you over, the Father's not against you, but for you, present in Christ to deliver you from your burdens. Where is bondage ultimately broken and rest forever gained? Look to the cross. *There* Christ proclaims the character and heart of God. Do we hear his good news of sheer grace by faith? Do we stand with straight backs by his mercy alone and glorify him for it? Do we rest wholly in the love of the Father who, through our light and momentary afflictions, is bringing us into his own everlasting rest?

CHAPTER 7

Being in the Spirit

What does it mean for us to live as sons and daughters adopted in the grace of God? In the last chapter, we pointed to the cross of Christ as the place where God's character and heart was displayed, where bondage is ultimately broken and rest forever gained. We said that the true test of a Christian was utter reliance upon the Father's goodness and faithfulness—a heart that's experienced God's deliverance, rests in him by faith, and for this reason exhibits a new perspective and a new ethic. In this chapter, we'll explore the reality of this new perspective and ethic—our life as Christians lived in the Spirit of God. Paul expresses the origin and nature of this life in Romans:

> There is therefore now no condemnation for those who are in Christ Jesus. For the law of the Spirit of life has set you free in Christ Jesus from the law of sin and death. For God has done what the law, weakened by the flesh, could not do. By sending his own Son in the likeness of sinful flesh and for sin, he condemned sin

in the flesh, in order that the righteous requirement of the law might be fulfilled in us, who walk not according to the flesh but according to the Spirit. For those who live according to the flesh set their minds on the things of the flesh, but those who live according to the Spirit set their minds on the things of the Spirit. For to set the mind on the flesh is death, but to set the mind on the Spirit is life and peace. For the mind that is set on the flesh is hostile to God, for it does not submit to God's law; indeed, it cannot. Those who are in the flesh cannot please God.

You, however, are not in the flesh but in the Spirit, if in fact the Spirit of God dwells in you. Anyone who does not have the Spirit of Christ does not belong to him. But if Christ is in you, although the body is dead because of sin, the Spirit is life because of righteousness. If the Spirit of him who raised Jesus from the dead dwells in you, he who raised Christ Jesus from the dead will also give life to your mortal bodies through his Spirit who dwells in you (Rom 8:1-11).

In one respect, the heart of that new perspective and ethic, what it means to live as sons and daughters, is summed up in verse 5: "For those who live according to the flesh set their minds on the things of the flesh, but those who live according to the Spirit set their minds on the things of the Spirit." (Here "flesh" refers to "sinful nature.") On one occasion John Owen said words to this effect: There are only two pastoral problems in the world. One is to convince men who are in sin, that they're in sin, and the other is to convince men who aren't in sin that they're not in sin.[1] In other words, to help folks see where they are presently at: Are they living according to the sinful nature, or according to rest in the Father?

Where Are We?

So where are you? Are you in the flesh or Spirit, that is, in sin or under grace? In Romans 8, like in many other places, Paul builds the application of his teaching around sets of dualities. For example, we're either in Adam, or in Christ. We're either under the law, or we're under grace. We're either dead, or alive. We're either condemned, or we're justified. We're either walking according to the prince of the power of this era, or we're sons and daughters of God. We're either darkness, or light. We're either in this present and expiring evil age, or we belong to the age to come that has broken into the present. We're either in the flesh, or in the Spirit.

Paul is not teaching, particularly in this matter of flesh and Spirit, that we're a mixture of both. It's not the case that you're in the Spirit when you're doing good works and in the flesh when you fail. We don't oscillate back and forth between being in the Spirit and being in the flesh. Paul is saying "no" categorically to such thinking. You're no longer in the flesh (in the sinful nature); he writes, "You … are not in the flesh but in the Spirit, if in fact the Spirit of God dwells in you" (Rom 8:9). In other words, if you're a Christian, you exist in the Spirit, plain and simple. You see things from a very different perspective. By the Spirit of God indwelling your life, driving the Word deep into your soul, he's opened your eyes, unstopped your ears, and given you a new heart. When Samuel anointed King Saul, he told him, "The Spirit of the Lord will rush upon you, and you will prophesy … and be turned into another man." Then "when he turned his back to leave Samuel, God gave him another heart" (1 Sam 10:6, 9). This is what being indwelt by the Holy Spirit looks like; it's hardly ever spectacular. Rather, it's a deep change of the heart, a reorientation, a new existence.

Therefore, in Paul's teaching the flesh and the Spirit are two opposing principles that represent two completely different states of being. The war that rages between the flesh and Spirit that is spoken of in Galatians—"For the desires of the flesh are against the Spirit, and the desires of the Spirit are against the flesh, for these are opposed to each other, to keep you from doing the things you want to do" (Gal 5:17)—isn't about defiled bodies and pure spirits; such an idea is gnostic. Rather, he's speaking of two different dominions, two different places of accountability. If you're in the flesh you belong to one realm of existence, and if you're in the Spirit you belong to another—namely, to God himself.

In the dominion of the flesh, there's lots of action: religion, worship, superstition, law, charity, and conscience, to name a few. On the surface it can look very similar to the dominion of the Spirit, and this is what makes it confusing. But life in the dominion of the flesh belongs to the old creation with all its religion, all of its so-called goodness, all of its self-righteousness, all of its expressions of human egotism. Fleshly existence can think it perfectly proper to justify a hard heart, such as critical tones of voice and facial expressions when wronged or denied justice. It becomes clear the so-called goodness was nothing more than a humanly manufactured product subconsciously focused on the self. This is why the flesh is under the sentence of condemnation, not the blessing of justification. To be in the flesh is still to be in Adam, not in Christ.

A common failure has been to think that the flesh can be transformed, that new rules, etiquette, and the will to put them into practice will make everything better, so God's commandments are taught with zeal. But the Scriptures object, the flesh can't be transformed. For it's a whole system bound to the old Adamic nature, a hostility and hatred that characterizes our murderous rage against God. Authentic transformation occurs only in the death of this nature and its inheritance of condemnation. And this is what has in fact occurred in the death and resurrection of Christ. In the Father's sending the Son into the world, he identified himself completely with Adam's doomed inheritance and put it to death at Calvary. The old nature is gone. A new nature was raised with Christ, and all who are in him by faith have been raised with him and live in his Spirit.

So the question is: Where are you? The flesh is a whole system of religious righteousness; it expresses itself across all cultures, across all religious systems. But it always works on the basis of you get what you deserve: *God helps those who help themselves; affliction's due to disobedience.* This is the flesh, not to the Spirit. But Christians are no longer in the flesh; they're in the Spirit. They're no longer in Adam; they're in Christ. They're no longer under condemnation; they've been justified. In other words, where you are can't be separated from the person in whom you stand.

When the message of our forgiveness truly captures our hearts, we're to realize the judgment against our old nature in Adam has been crucified with Christ and the accusation of the law against us has been abolished. God has made us alive in Christ, "having forgiven us all our trespasses, by canceling the record of debt that stood against us with its legal demands. This he set aside, nailing it to the cross" (Col 2:13-14). "There is therefore now no condemnation for those who are in Christ Jesus" (Rom 8:1).

The dominion of the flesh told you that you were related to God on the basis of what you do. But the dominion of the Spirit tells you that you are related to God on the basis of what he did—by faith, you stand in Christ. This is why the gospel is good news. The book of Romans is full of the message that we can't be God's sons and daughters on the basis of what we do. Why not? Because the law we strive so hard to obey only serves to show us our sin, to give us the knowledge of our condemnation. No matter how much we may do, our consciences never find peace. There's always something more to be done: Have our motives been sincere enough, have we done well enough often enough? The flesh can never rise to a justified state from within itself. The impure thing can never make itself pure. The law can't make us right with God. As Martin Luther once said, "The law says, 'do this,' and it is never done. Grace says, 'believe in this,' and everything is already done."[2]

As my (Noel's) first wife fought her battle with cancer we were mercifully freed from those accusations that said, "This has come upon us as punishment." God allowed us to know his grace, and allowed my wife in the most remarkable way to receive the freedom of it. What happened as Beverley came ever closer to the end goes against the textbooks. The books say as people come closer to the end of their life they become more insular and withdrawn, self-protective, anxious, and fearful. But the Lord opened up a river in her heart that flowed with love, joy, forgiveness, and peace right to the very last. Other patients, visitors, and family members were drawn into it. In the last week it was as though she was more in heaven than on earth. Such love and peace, however, doesn't come from the flesh. The flesh will always tell you your suffering is because of your sin. It will always tell you that the way you move close to God is on the basis of what you do, how well you do it, how often you do it, and with what motives you do it.

Our heavenly Father has purposed from all eternity to have a family of sons and daughters conformed to the image of his Son, Jesus Christ. He has sent his Son after us while we were still enemies (Rom 5:10), and this is an unthinkable act that the flesh could never comprehend because it doesn't understand grace. Christ doesn't stand off at a distance, saying, "When you've got your act together, you can come." He doesn't treat us according to the flesh. He treats us according to the Spirit of grace and love, saying, "I come to you." We don't deserve it. We can't earn it. We can't pay it back—even to try is to fall again into the error that we can please God by what we do—but "all our righteous deeds are like a polluted garment" (Isa 64:6). Our only response is worship, a gratitude swelling up from deep within a changed heart, a love for him that simply reflects his love for us. In Christ we have the Spirit of sonship, where before we were filled with the spirit of disobedience.

Where are you? The biggest battle you face throughout your entire Christian life, and you will have faced a thousand times today, is: "Am I in Christ?" When the world, and the flesh, and the devil, and the law in your own conscience accuse you, that battle is the battle of faith, to believe that where God has said you are is actually where you are. We are no longer in the flesh, if we are in Christ. "If anyone is in Christ, he is a new creation. The old has passed away; behold, the new has come" (2 Cor 5:17).

Who Are We?

Who are we? We are *sons* of God through union with Christ. Sonship is a status term; it's about positional reality. Men and women alike are sons of God; sonship applies without gender. It is blind to socioeconomic class, caste, race, or nationality. Those who by faith are united to Christ are sons of God.

The main point here, however, isn't actually the description of "sons" ("sons" here references position, not gender). Rather, it's what distinguishes us sons and daughters from the rest of humanity, namely, our union with Christ. This union occurs with our redemption. And redemption isn't based on what I say or do, but rather what I am as a person—whether I am in the truth (John 18:37). Being in the truth—what theologians call regeneration—is wholly dependent upon the words and works of Jesus Christ. We encounter Jesus in and through his words and works, which the Holy Spirit opens to us so we know him not as a dead historical figure with memorable quotes, but as God in whom there is life. The Spirit illuminates our hearts and minds to embrace the love of Christ as the truth; we answer his call in faith. By faith we grasp the deeper reality of the love of God in the life, death, and resurrection of Jesus. And this truth characterizes our reality, our experience of life and the world.

Union with Christ, then, is awakening to the recognition that we are creatures in desperate need of our Creator. And this occurs as his words and work are impressed upon our hearts by his Spirit. In regeneration our hearts recognize and embrace his love for us; we are in union with Christ; we are sons and daughters of God.

How do you know who you are? You know who you are by faith, because the Spirit bears witness with your spirit that you are indeed sons and daughters of God, that your sonship is true. In the very depths of your being, you have borne within your heart a cry that only a son or daughter of God may utter, the most beautiful, intimate, exalting, and dignifying cry creation could ever hear. It is the cry in your heart by which you sound out, "Abba! Father!" (Gal 4:6), simply communicating *God is my father*.

This is the same cry that appeared on Jesus' lips in the garden of Gethsemane (Mark 14:36). Therefore, the Spirit that was on him without measure has been given to you and me. It is the Spirit that unites the family of God with one voice crying, "Abba! Father!"

So where are you? If you know the truth of God, if you've seen in Christ his friendly heart, then you're no longer in the flesh, no longer in the old reality. You're in Christ and are a son or daughter of God.

Sometimes the cry of our hearts to God is barely a murmur. There are times, in perplexity and suffering, grief and sorrow, sin and failure, in the pain of life and all its complexities, when all you can do is sigh, "Father! Father!" Such a prayer might just be the most important and exalted prayer you've ever uttered. It's cleaving to Christ despite the silence of chaos that would seek to separate us from him. And there the Spirit carries us to the Father, for "we do not know what to pray for as we ought, but the Spirit himself intercedes for us with groanings too deep for words" (Rom 8:26).

An elderly man (whom Noel knew once) was visited at his door by an evangelist who asked the question: "Sir, are you afraid of dying?" His quick and matter of fact reply shocked the questioner: "Of course not. I died two thousand years ago." He was recounting his sonship. He'd died and been raised with Christ (cf. Rom 6:5–10; Col 3:1–3).

Where are we? We're in the state of having been justified through faith in Christ. We're in the state of being sanctified through faith in the loving-faithfulness of the Father through the Son by the Spirit. Who are we? We're sons of God in Jesus Christ. We're those who know the reality of God, who long for his face, ache for his touch, and utter with our lips, "Abba! Father!"

What Are We Waiting For?

What are we waiting for? Paul's answer is somewhat surprising. He says we're waiting for an unveiling:

> If then you have been raised with Christ, seek the things that are above, where Christ is, seated at the right hand of God. Set your minds on things that are above, not on things that are on earth. For you have died, and your life is hidden with Christ in God. When Christ who is your life appears, then you also will appear with him in glory (Col 3:1–4).

Paul is confident that the work God has accomplished in Jesus Christ is so settled and secure that nothing need be added to it. All that remains is for the outcome of this work, who we are, to be fully unveiled. Presently our identity is perceived through the eyes of faith—hidden in the heart of God. But seeing Christ face to face will transform us into his likeness, as we receive the fulfillment of his promise, our resurrection bodies (1 John 3:2; Rom 6:5). We will be at last what God intended us to be: sons and daughters fully trusting him as Father. But seeing by faith in this life now changes everything. Knowing who we are in Christ, finding our significance and security in the truth of his love for us, is the bedrock of our hope.

The forces of darkness that oppose God, however, also oppose us. And the battle that thunders has the obscuring of this fact as its sole purpose. To keep your true identity from you, to keep you in bondage to your story of suffering and sin, to tell you you're not a new creation, to convince you that God is not your Father, Lover, and Friend (Deut 23:5; Rom 8:39; John 15:15).

Because we are so quickly prone to fall into doubt and discouragement from the pressure of tribulation, danger, and distress, Paul points us to hope in the promises of God telling us that an unveiling, a revealing to sight, is coming: "The creation waits with eager longing for the revealing of the sons of God" (Rom 8:19). In Christ, who we are is fully settled and secure. There's nothing we don't already have in him, the fullness of the Father's loving-kindness, the wholeness of his blessings. The last day, then, is the pulling back of the curtain to reveal what already is. The hope that is ours against the world, the flesh, and the devil is the truth of God for us and the promise of his unveiling of our sonship (Rom 8:19, 31); this is what we are waiting for.

How Do We Wait?

How do we wait? We wait with faith, in hope, by love. The whole of the Christian life is summarized by these three words: faith, hope, and love. Through faith we are in Christ, eagerly "longing for the revealing of the sons of God" and the transformation of all of creation (Rom 8:19; cf. Rom 8:19–25), patiently persevering our present sufferings transfixed on the love of God for us (Rom 8:35).

What this means is that a movement is taking place in which the sons and daughters of the Father are being conformed to his image by being filled with the Father's love. Put differently, we do not yet completely grasp his love; it's the goal we're straining for (Phil 3:12–13), that which we are being perfected in (2 Cor 3:18). The roots of our life are to grow deeper and deeper into it (Jer 17:7–8), and yet this love of the Father has already been bestowed fully upon us in Christ Jesus, poured into our hearts by the Holy Spirit (Rom 5:5). No greater installment is forthcoming, only the unabridged unveiling of what has already been attained (1 Cor 13:12; Phil 3:16). This is the love that we are being conformed to, and "love is the fulfilling of the law" (Rom 13:10).

We live out our sonship in faith, hope, and love, for this is how Jesus lived his. "When he was reviled, he did not revile in return; when he suffered, he did not threaten, but continued entrusting himself to him who judges justly" (1 Pet 2:23). We don't need to walk in the paths of self-justification, which only breeds bitterness and hostility. We don't need to be endlessly arguing about who's right and who's wrong. We don't need to trust in our own strength to walk a better path than others, which turns our hearts away from the Lord (Jer 17:5). Our actions are transformed not by sheer will, but by entrusting ourselves to God who is our Father and who keeps us in his love (Jer 17:7). This is what we were referring to in the last chapter. The mark of our Christian life is our response to all of life. Do we keep entrusting ourselves vulnerably to the Father? As we trust his character, that is, his sovereignty, goodness and loving-kindness towards us, we cannot but be changed, bearing fruit as the life of the vine flows through us (John 15:5).

I (Noel) once heard a tale about a man on a desert island who'd been there by himself. After several years a steamer came past, saw his signal fire, and rescued him. When the tender came out from the steamer, he ran across the beach, and the guys on the tender noticed three buildings behind him and asked him what they were for. The castaway responded, "That's my house, that's the church I go to every Sunday, and the one next to it is the church I'll never go to, ever!" In so many ways we can be so self-righteous, so right about a particular issue, that we're dead wrong.

Because of our justification in Christ, because God's removed the condemnation from us and declares and accepts us as his beloved sons and daughters, he rejoices over us with gladness and quiets us with his love (Zeph 3:17). He doesn't come to us in a halfhearted way. He doesn't do an "elder brother" on us, standing back with pride and contempt, asserting his own righteousness and criticizing us (Luke 15:25–30). Rather, he comes himself and brings out the robe of honor. He clothes us with Christ, he stands us in Christ, placing us in the bosom of his beloved Son who is in his own very bosom. In other words, the Father himself embraces us and brings us into himself through his work of removing the judgments against us in Christ. This is the Church's dwelling place eternally. This is why Paul says:

> Neither death nor life, nor angels nor rulers, nor things present nor things to come, nor powers, nor height nor depth, nor anything else in all creation, will be able to separate us from the love of God in Christ Jesus our Lord (Rom 8:38-39).

Walking by faith, living by faith, being sanctified by faith, means coming back to this reality over and over and over again. Dwelling on it. Lingering on it. Allowing it to move us and to have its effect on us at the deepest and most fundamental level. This is what Paul prays for in Ephesians:

> I bow my knees before the Father, from whom every family in heaven and on earth is named, that according to the riches of his glory he may grant you to be strengthened with power through his Spirit in your inner being, so that Christ may dwell in your hearts through faith—that you, being rooted and grounded in love, may have strength to comprehend with all the saints what is the breadth and length and height and depth, and to know the love of Christ that surpasses knowledge, that you may be filled with all the fullness of God (Eph 3:14-19).

What about affliction, however? What about the pressures of the world? What about suffering we experience as expectations of others are heaped upon us, as we experience unfathomable loss or cruelty? What about the real felt pain of all of this? None of it changes the gospel. And it doesn't change the fact that we're able to endure all such struggles only in straining to hear the gospel and cleaving to it. It's only by abandoning ourselves to trust in the character of God, which the gospel proclaims, that we see those struggles, no matter how arduous, as light momentary afflictions.

The devil would love to tell you that the affliction, suffering, or pain we experience is proof of the fact that we aren't loved, that we aren't in Christ, that either we are being punished or forgotten about, or that God just isn't there at all. He desires that you'd come to the point of believing that living by faith is a farce. But there's no truth in him, for he's the father of lies (John 8:44).

You are no longer in the flesh; you're in Christ Jesus. You're no longer a son or daughter of disobedience under judgment of the broken law, but are justified by the blood of Christ, standing under the full blessing of the Father's love, never to be turned away. This is who you are, this is your identity. The world doesn't see it, and you may often forget it, but it is secure in the Father's heart. And we are waiting for the time in which the veil will be pulled back and our faith and identity will give way to sight as we look upon the one in whom we have believed. Therefore, we wait with hope, longing for our Lord, living now in light of our sonship—living in the obedience of faith, which is love, which alone fills the law (Luke 10:27; Rom 13:8; Gal 5:6).

CHAPTER 8

Walking in the Spirit

The activity of the Holy Spirit is of great significance, especially in a book about our coming to know God as Father. For it's through the Father's gift of the Spirit that we're enabled to call intimately upon him with the cry, "Abba! Father!" (Gal 4:6). Throughout this book there's been a Trinitarian current, in that in speaking about the work of the Father we've had to speak in the same breath about the work of the Son and Spirit. So in this chapter our focus will be on the Holy Spirit who brings us into the experience of the fullness of the Father's life.

The story line of salvation history includes God's tearing down walls of hostility between people, beginning with the barrier between Jew and Gentile (Eph 2:11-12). He's done this by making them one people through the blood of Christ (Eph 2:13) — fulfilling the promise to Abraham that in him all the families of the earth would be blessed (Gen 12:3). As one "holy temple in the Lord" they grow together as a "dwelling place for God by the Spirit" (Eph 2:21-22). For God "does not live in temples made by man, nor is he served by human hands, as though he needed anything, since he himself gives to all mankind life and breath and everything" (Acts 17:24-25). Rather, he dwells in the Church, that is, he dwells in the people whom he's called to himself and united to his Son by the Spirit. This astonishing reality shouldn't be missed! God intimately makes his home in our hearts, filling them with his presence. And this is what the activity of the Holy Spirit is all about: *that our life should be nothing other than the life of the Son in the Father* (John 5:21, 26; 14:11).

But we struggle to comprehend what this "life of the Son" is, how we enter it, and how we go about living in it. It sounds a bit esoteric. We might be helped, however, by a few poor analogies. Like electricity that gives life to a power cable, or a sporting event that gives rise to the spirited mood of a crowd, so the Father fills Christ with the fullness of his life, i.e., his truth and character. And when Christ sends the Holy Spirit into our hearts—his Church—he fills the world with the fullness of the Father's life (Eph 4:10). In other words, by the Spirit we participate in God's own life, just as a mirror participates in the light shown in it.

At the top of all this is the fact that the fullness of life is in God alone—God is full of himself (Psa 16:11). Usually to say that one is full of him or herself isn't a compliment. It brings to mind a picture of an egotistical, self-centered, ambitious, and proud person. But applied to God, it means he has no unmet needs. He doesn't act to fill a need for security or significance. In contrast, when we have unmet needs we try to fill them with a variety of things. But nothing within God needs to be filled; he's already complete and therefore free of need.

It's this very freedom that we all are called to participate in. The Apostle Paul writes in Galatians, "You were called to freedom, brothers. Only do not use your freedom as an opportunity for the flesh, but through love serve one another" (5:13). What he's saying is we ought not turn our freedom from the law's condemnation, into an opportunity to serve ourselves, in order to fill ourselves. Why? Because to be free is to be complete. The fullness that God has in himself isn't a self-directed fullness, but a complete freedom by which he's able to be for us. In other words, in creating and redeeming us he's not trying to bolster his ego or find approval to fill an unmet need.

The Law and the Gospel

Because it's so often misunderstood we need to linger here. The freedom we have *from* the law of God isn't a freedom from its perfection and righteousness (Psa 19:7–8; Rom 7:12), but from its condemnation (Rom 8:1). God's law declares to us the holy and righteous character of God, mirroring what we ought to be but aren't, holding us accountable (Rom 3:19). It's often mistakenly understood, however, that Jesus nullified the law, removed our need to be accountable to it. But this is the farthest thing from the truth—hear his own words:

> Do not think that I have come to abolish the Law or the Prophets; I have not come to abolish them but to fulfill them. For truly, I say to you, until heaven and earth pass away, not an iota, not a dot, will pass from the Law until all is accomplished (Matt 5:17–18).

Since the law of God remains in effect, we can't ignore it. We should see, however, that in terms of the plan of salvation it has one purpose and one only: "[T]hrough the law comes knowledge of sin" (Rom 3:20). In other words, its purpose is to convict us of our sinfulness (Rom 3:23)—which is our failure to love God (Matt 22:37)—and drive us to the gospel of Christ to experience his love and redemption from the penalty of the broken law (Rom 3:24). Does the law teach us what holiness looks like? It does indeed because it announces the character of God. Yet striving after obedience to the law doesn't make us holy. "For by works of the law no human being will be justified in [God's] sight" (Rom 3:20). Rather, Paul directs us to strive after the one place in which we're made holy, the one place our hard hearts are actually enabled to love God as we ought (Phil 3:8-16): *the loving-faithful-ness of God in Jesus Christ—the gospel.*

Only Jesus has obeyed the law perfectly in love for God and man. In receiving his grace, the Father justifies us and creates in us a love for himself—we can love God only when we're overwhelmed by his love for us. Hence, our love reflects his. Endeavoring to justify ourselves before God and others through obedience to the law never leads us to love God or others (Matt 22:37-40). Rather, it leads us into boasting and self-righteousness when we succeed—which breaks the law (1 Cor 1:29)—or beneath the crushing weight of guilt and shame when we fail. Only the gospel has the ability to lead us into love. This is why Paul writes:

> The law of the Spirit of life has set you free in Christ Jesus from the law of sin and death. For God has done what the law, weakened by the flesh, could not do. By sending his own Son in the likeness of sinful flesh and for sin, he condemned sin in the flesh, in order that the righteous requirement of the law might be fulfilled in us, who walk not according to the flesh but according to the Spirit. For those who live according to the flesh set their minds on the things of the flesh, but those who live according to the Spirit set their minds on the things of the Spirit (Rom 8:2-4).
>
> He is the source of your life in Christ Jesus, whom God made our wisdom and our righteousness and sanctification and redemption. Therefore, as it is written, "Let the one who boasts, boast in the Lord" (1 Cor 1:30-31).

What we're to set our minds on and what we're to boast in, therefore, is the same thing: *the loving-faithfulness of God in Jesus Christ—the gospel.*

When the gospel isn't at the center of one's faith—that is, when one loses sight of God's love—he or she will fall into one of two ditches. The first we can describe as the "happy moralist," and the second as the "sad moralist."[1]

The happy moralist is convinced that God loves them, that's he's obligated to do so, as well as to bless them when they do good. They know he has some rules, but these can be reduced to a few duties, which one generally assumes they're doing rather well at. Jesus harshly criticized happy moralists, contrasting their outward show of religion with their neglect of "the weightier matters of the law" (Matt 23:23), which speaks to issues of what is going on in the heart—justice, mercy, and faithfulness—and points out issues such as greed, self-indulgence, pride, hypocrisy, lawlessness, etc. In other words, the happy moralist doesn't take the law personally and seriously enough, even while they might be overly scrupulous and even add works to faith. Such superficial law keeping, however, is another way of avoiding the humiliation intrinsic to entrusting themselves to the gospel—that is, seeing themselves as deeply sinful and in need of grace. The happy moralist doesn't fully see how the law applies to them, and they actually feel they're pretty good. Yet they're easily irritated, judgmental, and find it difficult to receive criticism. They're the Pharisee (Matt 23:1–36). Martin Luther admonished the happy moralist as follows:

> You must get this thought through your head and not doubt that you are the one who is torturing Christ thus, for your sins have surely wrought this. ... Therefore, when you see the nails piercing Christ's hands, you can be certain it is your work. When you behold his crown of thorns, you may rest assured that these are your evil thoughts.[2]

The sad moralists experience the weight of God's law. They aren't fooled into thinking they're doing well in fulfillment of it. In fact, they're very much aware of how much they're failing and feel they ought to be doing better. The sad moralists are quite harsh with themselves, thrashing themselves with condemnation and doubling their efforts to obey. Trying to justify themselves through repentance, their consciences never find peace.

Finally exhausted, they give in to apathy and self-indulgence, only to start the cycle of self-reformation over again. When the sad moralists read of God's love for them in Christ, they aren't comforted, but terrified; the joy of the gospel hasn't infected their heart. Sad moralists, like happy moralists, also avoid the gospel, albeit differently. They avoid it by trying to prove they are worthy of God's love and blessings by relying on their own righteousness. They look on others who seem to be enjoying God's blessings with contempt because they aren't working hard enough; they're censorious, envious, and can be hateful of Christians with weak or different theology. They're the elder brother in the parable of the prodigal son (Luke 15:11-32). George Whitefield admonished the sad moralist as follows:

> Our best duties are as so many splendid sins. Before you can speak peace to your heart you must not only be sick of your original and actual sin, but you must be made sick of your righteousness, of all your duties and performances. There must be a deep conviction before you can be brought out of your self-righteousness; it is the last idol taken out of your heart. The pride of the heart will not let us submit to the righteousness of Jesus Christ.[3]

And David Brainerd, 18th-century missionary to the Native Americans, wrote:

> When I had been fasting, praying, obeying, I thought I was aiming at the glory of God, but I was doing it all for my own glory—to feel I was worthy. As long as I was doing all this to earn my salvation, I was doing nothing for God, all for me! I realized that all my struggling to become worthy was an exercise in self-worship. I was not worshipping him, but using him. ... Though I often confessed to God that I, of course, deserved nothing, yet still I harbored a secret hope of recommending myself

to God by all these duties and all this morality. In other words, I healed myself with my duties.[4]

Walking in the Spirit

When the gospel frees us from the condemnation of the law, it also frees us from the need to create our own sense of identity by garnering acceptance, approval, and love from others, or producing our own sense of importance and significance through our actions. It also means we can't recommend ourselves to God. Because God meets our needs in the gospel, bringing us into his freedom by the Holy Spirit, we're free to move towards each other in love. As we've said, God's own fullness enables him to move towards us freely in love. And as we come to experience the depth of that love, we're filled with his Spirit whose fruit—love, joy, peace, patience, kindness, goodness, faithfulness, gentleness, and self-control—is displayed in our lives (Gal 5:22-23).

In the sublime figure of Michelangelo's David hewn from solid marble we can appreciate the skill, creativity, and determination that went into bringing it to life. We can see its detail and stand in awe that such a thing could be accomplished with a hammer and chisel. Yet, however much the statue displays Michelangelo's skill, it is not his flesh and blood. It doesn't flow with his spirit. It's a static representation of something. The statue can never turn to Michelangelo and say, "I love you." It can never open its arms and embrace him. And while Michelangelo might pour his life out over it, he could never fill it with his life. It will always remain a made thing.

Christians aren't made, they're born of the Spirit of God to be what a made thing could never be (John 3:5-6)—namely, filled with the life of the Father. Of course, God is our maker, but not in a static sense. He's dynamically active through re-creation, or new birth, through the person of the Spirit, so that we might be filled with and reflect his love. We know the Father only through the work of his loving-kindness upon us in the Son and Spirit.

That is, we know him only as we're overcome by the message of the gospel.

In the Letter to the Galatians, Paul can't speak about the main theme of justification without also speaking about the Holy Spirit. The reason for this is that justification has to do with a right standing before God, which means love for God. Righteousness, peace, joy, and love for God can't be gained through the law. What's needed is a radical change of heart that only the Spirit of God can bring about by acquainting us with God's own love for us in Christ's work at Calvary. There "Christ redeemed us from the curse of the law by becoming a curse for us—for it is written, 'Cursed is everyone who is hanged on a tree' " (Gal 3:13). This truth is followed in the next verse by two purpose clauses: "So that in Christ Jesus the blessing of Abraham might come to the Gentiles, so that we might receive the promised Spirit through faith" (Gal 3:14). In other words, redemption targets the nations for blessing by the giving of the Holy Spirit, which is the begetting of love for and fullness in the Father. This point is repeated in the next chapter:

> But when the fullness of time had come, God sent forth his Son, born of woman, born under the law, to redeem those who were under the law, so that we might receive adoption as sons. And because you are sons, God has sent the Spirit of his Son into our hearts, crying, "Abba! Father!" (Gal 4:4–6).

Why is the Spirit significant to the nations? Because apart from the sending of the Son and Spirit, individuals, and so nations, live under the law and its curse in which the works of the flesh are evident: "sexual immorality, impurity, sensuality, idolatry, sorcery, enmity, strife, jealousy, fits of anger, rivalries, dissensions, divisions, envy, drunkenness, orgies, and things like these" (Gal 5:19–21). Peace only comes to individuals, and so nations, when they stop walking according to the law and flesh and come to walk according to love and the Spirit. It is only through life in the Spirit that we see the kingdom of God; that is, realize the love of the Father and realize "love, joy, peace, patience, kindness, goodness, faithfulness, gentleness, self-control" among us as sons and daughters of God (Gal 5:22–23). Justification, therefore, has at its heart the radical changing of our hearts through love for the purpose of freeing us to love.

Imagine if idolatry, enmity, strife, jealousy, fits of anger, rivalries, dissensions, divisions, and envy were removed from the world's political processes, from the church, from your family, from your own heart. The world would be a different place. Well, in Psalm 46 God says:

> Come, behold the works of the Lord,
> > how he has brought desolations on the earth.
> He makes wars cease to the end of the earth;
> > he breaks the bow and shatters the spear;
> > he burns the chariots with fire.
> "Be still, and know that I am God.
> > I will be exalted among the nations,
> > I will be exalted in the earth!" (Psa 46:8–10)

This is mighty work, indeed! How does God make wars cease? How does he make war to cease between you and your neighbors, your kids, your spouse, even within your own heart? He does it by delivering us from the domain of darkness and transferring us to the kingdom of his beloved Son (Col 1:13), so that we would not walk according to the flesh, but being filled with the Father himself through his Spirit, find our lives directed in love towards service of one another (Gal 5:13). Not being "conceited, provoking one another, envying one another" (Gal 5:26), not taking our own vengeance, not repaying "evil for evil or reviling for reviling" (1 Pet 3:9) because we're cleaving to God who has completed us—we're no longer slaves but sons and daughters (Gal 4:7).

There is no power whatsoever in our fleshly will to walk like this. When we try to walk on mere commitments to follow the law, to use Jesus as a mere example, we find it impossible and slip into either happy or sad moralism. But Jesus isn't a new Moses; the gospel isn't a new law. Rather, Jesus gains our justification and sends his Spirit "into our hearts, crying, 'Abba! Father!' " (Gal 4:6). When we truly know God as Father through his Spirit, we are free to trust and rest in him, and his fruit is evident in our lives.

Hearing with Faith

How do we receive the Spirit? How do we walk in the fullness of the Spirit? The answer to these two important questions is the same: We receive and walk in the Spirit *by hearing with faith*. Note what Paul says to the Galatians, "O foolish Galatians! Who has bewitched you? It was before your eyes that Jesus Christ was publicly portrayed as crucified. Let me ask you only this: Did you receive the Spirit by works of the law or *by hearing with faith*?" (3:1–2). And when Peter was speaking in Cornelius's home "the Holy Spirit fell on all who heard the word" (Acts 10:44). We receive and walk in the Spirit, therefore, by hearing with faith.

When the Holy Spirit is working on us, God's Word changes us. As we spoke in the last chapter, becoming true hearers of the Word brings us into a new atmosphere in which our questions, concerns, thoughts, hopes, feelings, and experiences are viewed and understood in light of Christ. It's a new existence, which has its origin in the work of the gospel upon them. Try as we might we can't change our own hearts. But the Spirit can as he carries the gospel deep into them and gives us ears to hear. When the walls of our hearts are torn down and our ears unstopped in grasping God's love for us, we'll discover in a momentary glance backward that we're walking in the Spirit (1 John 1:7).

Here's also, however, the problem we have in walking in the Spirit, why his fruit is often missing from our words and actions: *We don't really grasp God's love for us.* Put differently, we don't fully believe that he sees us, that he cares for us, that he is leading us, that he is defending us, that he is providing for us, that he is the single answer to all we need. Because of our individual stories of pain and suffering we chase after different things to have our needs met. Situations and circumstances tend to push us into the ruts of deeply worn habits of protecting and fending for ourselves. Turning to God in faith and trusting vulnerably in who he is for us is an afterthought, if a thought at all. And yet it's God alone who is complete—only he can fill us with what we need— namely, himself.

There's no power or ability to walk in the Spirit by our own strength and will, because when we walk alone we're not filled or freed to love others. There's something we're seeking to have met, some personal need for respect, approval, acceptance, significance, etc. Only when we're filled with God himself, grasping the gospel, are all such needs met, and we're free to walk in love. If the fruit of the Spirit isn't reflected in our walk, the answer isn't doubling our efforts. Rather, the answer is to hear the gospel. Often this may include confessing and releasing an idol we've latched onto instead of the truth of God for us. We might even need the help of a friend or pastor to see that idol. But unless we own it, confess it, and ask God's forgiveness for it, it remains a barrier blocking us from hearing God's love for us in that area. In fact, in the very act of repentance, we experience God's song of grace over us, and this changes us (Zeph 3:17).

The Holy Spirit is received by hearing the gospel with faith. Faith is born through hearing, and we're caught up into the life, character, emotion, and mood of God himself. And what we're to hear with faith is the gospel of Jesus Christ, which is a true and tangible demonstration of a simpler point we can't afford to miss—namely, that God loves us, cares for us, and is faithful to us. We've got to hear Calvary sounding the loving-faithfulness of God. For only in hearing this do our hearts come in the present moment to possess our sonship. Only in remembering the *loving-faithfulness of the Father* in the midst of our tribulations, temptations, tensions, and anxieties are they replaced by peace and joy.

Too often, however, we hear something else: "God's taken the first move in sending Christ, but now the rest is up to you. He'll be checking in on you for the rest of your days, checking the activities of your hands and heart. So you'd better work hard. Pay him back. Show him you're thankful." It's no different from our concluding the chapter by challenging you to commit yourself to godly living. Either your ego would respond positively, or you'd be shamed into action, but either way you'd be back under the curse of the law, without the experience of joy, peace, and love inhabiting your heart.

But if you hear the gospel in faith, then you hear that the fullness of God is for you. For the gospel of grace is the message of God's love; it's his drawing you as a son or daughter to know and trust him as Father. Your sin is deeper and more subtle than you realize, but the loving-faithfulness of God is also deeper than you realize. There's nothing left for you to do; it's all been sorted out at Calvary. Anything outside of going deeper into the realization of this truth is of the flesh and bears no fruit, for it's not connected to the life of God (John 15:4–5). We walk in the Spirit, exhibiting the fruit of the Spirit, only when we are filled with the Spirit, that is, filled with the love of the Father by hearing with faith.

Charles Spurgeon concludes well the power of the gospel we must hear and its power to do what the law cannot.

> The law commands love, indeed all its precepts are summed up in that word love. The more widely read it runs thus, thou shalt love the Lord thy God with all thy heart and with all thy soul, and with all thy strength, and with all thy mind, and thy neighbor as thy self. Yet all of this amounts to thou shalt love. But the law, by reason of our depravity never produced love. We were commanded to love, but we did no such thing. The spirit which is our normal fallen human spirit, is selfish and it runs to envy and to enmity. So where come wars and fightings amongst us, do they not come from our lusts and desires in the flesh? Since the fall man has become

man's bitterest enemy on the earth the world is full of hating, slander, struggling, fighting, woundings, slaying, and all the law could do was to show us the wrong and threaten punishment but it cannot supply the unregenerate with a fountain of love. Man remains unloving and unloveable till the gospel takes him in hand and by grace it accomplishes that which the law could not do, in that it was weak through the flesh. Love is winning many hearts to the kingdom of God. And its reign shall extend till love shall reign over the whole earth, so that the kingdom of God shall be set up amongst men and God will dwell among them.[5]

CHAPTER 9

Confident Access

All creation has its roots in God. So on one hand he's the father of all—every man and woman is his offspring and receives gifts of kindness and mercy. "For he makes his sun rise on the evil and the good, and sends rain on the just and unjust" (Matt 5:45). And yet on the other hand, his fatherhood isn't known to all. A great grace accompanies the act of adoption in which we come to know that God is indeed our Father, that we have access to him. It's this idea of access that is our concern in this chapter.

"Access" is a significant theme in the book of Ephesians. Even while the term itself is mentioned only a couple times, it appears at very crucial points, such as in Ephesians 2:

> He came and preached peace to you who were far off and peace to those who were near. For through him we both have access in one Spirit to the Father (2:17-18).

Paul is speaking here of God's plan of redemption to bring Jew and Gentile alike into Christ to "have access in one Spirit to the

Father." The removal of hostility and the making of peace both between one another and God occurs in his including us in his household (Eph 2:14, 16). "So then you are no longer strangers and aliens, but you are fellow citizens with the saints and members of the household of God," says Paul (Eph 2:19).

This is the mysterious plan and purpose of God—to build for himself a holy temple from all peoples—and why Paul was called "to preach to the Gentiles the unsearchable riches of Christ" (Eph 3:8). But he also preaches "so that through the church the manifold wisdom of God might now be made known to the rulers and authorities in the heavenly places" (Eph 3:10). In other words, the gospel cosmically broadcasts the divine mystery, which centers on and culminates in our *access* to the Father.

> This was according to the eternal purpose that he has realized in Christ Jesus our Lord, in whom we have boldness and access with confidence through our faith in him (Eph 3:11-12).

Before we consider the meaning of such access, however, we need to look closely at to whom this access is given. For to whom we have access makes all the difference to our understanding of its meaning and basis.

To Whom We Have Access

Paul's mentioning of access to God the Father in the verses above is set within the context of two significant statements. In the first chapter of Ephesians, he's emphasized God's eternal plan to bestow spiritual blessing through adopting us into Jesus Christ in whom "we have redemption though his blood, the forgiveness of our trespasses, according to the riches of his grace" (Eph 1:7). Why? So that all things in heaven and earth would be united, we would possess the inheritance and hope to which he has called us, and Christ would be established as head over all things to the glory of the Father (Eph 1:10, 12, 18, 22).

This great story of God encapsulates our individual stories. As hard as it is sometimes to comprehend and accept, nothing happens in our lives, or even in the history of the nations, which isn't encompassed in this plan and purpose of the Father to glorify himself in the Son by settling the whole of creation under his lordship, so all would exalt him (Phil 2:9–11; cf. Isa 45:23). This is the first statement that forms the context of our "access."

We've already alluded to the second statement. It's the removal of ethnic divides and making of peace, the creation of one new humanity in the place of two (Eph 2:15), through reconciliation in the cross of Jesus Christ. In other words, being in Christ means we're in a place we weren't before. Before this, we were strangers to the covenants of promise, cut off from God, without hope in the world. We weren't sons and daughters of God but were sons and daughters of disobedience under wrath. "But God, being rich in mercy, because of the great love with which he loved us, even when we were dead in our trespasses, made us alive together with Christ" (Eph 2:4–5). It has been said that mercy means you don't get what you deserve, and grace that you freely get what you've never earned. And so in becoming objects of God's redeeming mercy and grace in faith we experience in our hearts "the love of Christ that surpasses knowledge" (Eph 3:19).

Paul's discussion of the Father to whom we have access is set within the context of the goal of creation and redemption: *the Father's glorification because of his love through the Son.*

Redemption in the love of the Father is linked with the word adoption. The redeemed are those who've been adopted in Christ. J. I. Packer writes:

> God adopts us out of His free love, not because our character and record shows us worthy to bear his name, but despite the fact that they show the opposite. We are not fit for a place in God's family; the idea of His loving and exalting us sinners as he loves and has exalted the Lord Jesus sounds ludicrous and wild—yet that and nothing less than that, is what our adoption means.[1]

Access to the Father is the fruit of our adoption. "For this reason," Paul says, "I bow my knees before the Father, from whom every family in heaven and on earth is named" (Eph 3:14-15). The nature of God's fatherhood is reflected in our human families, for even in their imperfection the family is the typical place for nurture and direction (the church, organizations, and companies commonly function as surrogate families). God's fatherhood, which loves and redeems, is experienced and recognized in relational life.

Paul, however, also sees the family in terms of citizenship, writing, "For through [Christ] we both have access in one Spirit to the Father. So then you are no longer strangers and aliens, but you are *fellow citizens* with the saints and members *of the household of God*" (Eph 2:18-19). In other words, from his own background as a Roman citizen, Paul perceives an additional dimension of the one whom we have access to. Undoubtedly he sees the Father as the protector of those who abide in him—this is the theme of Psalm 91.

> He who dwells in the shelter of the Most High
> > will abide in the shadow of the Almighty.
> I will say to the Lord, "My refuge and my fortress,
> > my God, in whom I trust." ...
> Because you have made the Lord your dwelling place—
> > the Most High, who is my refuge—
> no evil shall be allowed to befall you,
> > no plague come near your tent. ...
> Because he holds fast to me in love, I will deliver him;
> > I will protect him, because he knows my name.
> When he calls to me, I will answer him;
> > I will be with him in trouble;
> > I will rescue him and honor him (Psa 91:1-2, 9-10, 14-15).

In Roman society, the father of the family not only managed his own children, but also ruled over the entire estate, which often included servants, slaves, and those seeking refuge and shelter. Hence the Roman father serves as a powerful image of the way in which God the Father takes responsibility over his household, how he manages and protects it for the fulfillment of his plan and purpose.

Throughout history we've expected fathering from our political leaders. Dictators have promised such, and emperors have called themselves such. The Roman emperor even bore the title of *pater patriae*, meaning, "Father of the Fatherland." We imagine Paul speaking to the Ephesians in effect saying: "You're a mixed lot. Some of you are Jews, some are Roman citizens, some are barbarian, some are Scythian, some are slaves, some are male, some are female, but all of you are sons and daughters of a great Father. And so your destiny isn't bound to the estate rules; your identity isn't defined by your history or status. It doesn't rest in the hands of the emperor, who, claiming the title of father, might yet turn against you. No matter how deep your personal story of suffering, no matter if persecution breaks out against you and your life is lost, you're an heir of God, and he's planned for you before the beginning of time. He guarantees your security and gives himself as your hope. You've access to the true Father."

The emperor doesn't trump the fatherhood of God. Your employer doesn't trump the fatherhood of God. The elders in your church don't trump the fatherhood of God. Your own father, who may have been adequate or inadequate, doesn't trump the fatherhood of God. God's fatherhood is secure; it's loving-faithfulness; it's full of mercy and grace, full of nurture, direction, protection, and provision. This is the character and love of the Father that we can trust, and why Paul bows his knees before him (Eph 3:14). To quote again from J. I. Packer:

> God receives us as sons, and loves us with the same steadfast affection with which He eternally loves His beloved only-begotten. There are no distinctions of affection in the divine family. We are all loved just as fully as Jesus is loved. ... This, and nothing less than this, is what adoption means. No wonder that John cries,

"Behold, what manner of love...!" When once you understand adoption, your heart will cry the same.[2]

The Meaning of Access

Our adoption grants us access to this loving Father. But what's so special about access?

As we've seen, Paul has spoken in Ephesians 2:11–22 about the barrier between people having been removed, because sin—which is the barrier between God and us—has been removed in the cross of Christ. Therefore, people of different socioeconomic, cultural, and ethnic backgrounds are joined together "into a holy temple in the Lord" by virtue of their having "access in one Spirit to the Father" (Eph 2:22, 18).

A special thing this accessibility to God grants is worship—that is, entrance into the holy of holies. Such access was always denied to Gentiles and ritually unclean Jews. The closest they could get was behind the wall of the temple's outer court. The Jewish people had access themselves to the holy of holies, but only through the priests, not in their own right. They would bring their sacrifice to the altar of holocaust (burnt offering) and wait there while the priests took it into the temple. But even then access to the holy of holies was off limits. Only the high priest entered once a year on the Day of Atonement to burn incense and sprinkle sacrificial animal blood to make amends for his own sins and those of the people of Israel.

So Paul's claim is preposterous coming from a highly educated and zealous Pharisee. Because Christ Jesus has fully atoned for your sin, you can go with confidence into the place accessible only by the high priest (Heb 10:19). Yet the place the high priest entered was a mere earthly copy of the true thing in heaven (Heb 9:24), and this is what we have full access into. Through the grace of God's own loving-kindness, his provision of the spotless lamb of Christ Jesus, he has brought us into the true holy of holies, his very presence.

Without access to his presence, we're lost, cut off from his love, without life. For this reason the psalmist prays, "In your steadfast love give me life" (Psa 119:88). He realizes that only within the presence of God's loving-kindness is true peace and life found. So he cries out to God from the depths of his crisis, and this is his act of worship—he fastens himself to the Father, to his protection, and waits for his deliverance. Which brings us to another reason why access is special.

We've already noted how Paul connects access with citizenship. A Roman citizen had rights not given to others—for example, the protection of the Emperor as the *pater patriae* ("Father of the Fatherland"). Paul claimed this when he was about to be questioned under torture:

> When they had stretched him out for the whips, Paul said to the centurion who was standing by, "Is it lawful for you to flog a man who is a Roman citizen and uncondemned?" When the centurion heard this, he went to the tribune and said to him, "What are you about to do? For this man is a Roman citizen." So the tribune came and said to him, "Tell me, are you a Roman citizen?" And he said, "Yes." The tribune answered, "I bought this citizenship for a large sum." Paul said, "But I am a citizen by birth." So those who were about to examine him withdrew from him immediately, and the tribune also was afraid, for he realized that Paul was a Roman citizen and that he had bound him (Acts 22:25-29).

As aliens and exiles, those previously without citizenship, we now have access to the great Father, to his nurture, care, provision, and protection. We need such access, because each day we are standing in a law court with a desperately hostile witness, the devil, who hurls lies at us causing us to believe we're utterly unacceptable to God, that we're outside his care and protection, that we're not sons and daughters. But we are! Our adoption into Christ has made it so. Our birth in the Spirit of God has opened our hearts to see and hear the truth of God in Christ Jesus, so we have the mind of Christ and cry, "Abba! Father!" (1 Cor 2:16; Gal 4:6).

Our sonship means the Father is available to us, that we're acceptable to him no matter how we feel. Jesus declared just this type of access when he said, "No longer do I call you servants, for the servant does not know what his master is doing; but I have called you friends, for all that I have heard from my Father I have made known to you" (John 15:15). This is why access is so special; it implies certainty of acceptance, provision, and protection.

The Basis of Access

Our access, however, is granted with a face, not a book—not even a prayer book. Sonship isn't experienced on the basis of religious protocol, morality, or tradition. It's gained and experienced in the love communicated through Christ.

Paul's letters are full of phrases that include the words "in Christ," "with Christ," "through Christ," and "by Christ." Ephesians contains 15 or so phrases. The point is we have nothing apart from Christ, but "in him we have obtained an inheritance" (Eph 1:11). This inheritance is full access to, full availability of, and full acceptance by the Father. In other words, the Father "has blessed us in Christ with every spiritual blessing in the heavenly places" (Eph 1:3). In Christ we have entrance into the holy of holies, and a citizenship that cannot be revoked. Through Christ we have a father who always has his ear bent to hear the silent cries of our spirits, "Abba! Father!"

You have the Father. You don't approach him on the basis of protocol or your own perfection; you approach in confidence because Christ is there and, by faith, you're in Christ. Since your access to God isn't based on what you do but wholly based on what Christ has done, it can't be lost. In other words, Christ has secured our access to the presence of the Father. And this is where we are.

From the beginning of creation through to its end, the Father holds us in the loving-kindness of his own heart revealed to us in

Christ. This is our identity: We're secured by the Son, sealed by the Spirit, and hidden in the heart of the Father.

There are times we're prone to forget our access to God, to be utterly confused about our identity. There are times when we find ourselves in the darkest holes, in the most perplexing situations, surrounded by the most dire circumstances. We can't see the reality of our identity, nor can the world around us see it, but this doesn't change its truth one bit. The German Lutheran theologian, Helmut Thielicke, puts it well:

> An identity is ascribed to us that is grounded in God's history with us. Hence this identity is independent of our condition at any given time. ... Even as one who has become new in God's grace, even as a "new creature," I still look back on what I was, on that other element in me (Romans 7:14ff.), and I realize that in the mind of God I live in two ways, first, as the one whose old life, whose "old Adam," he knows well, and then as the one whom he embraces in his mercy, justifies, and accepts.[3]

No matter how we feel, we remain a son or daughter of the Father because of his love for us in Christ (John 3:16–17). Our sonship, therefore, isn't based on our perception or experience of it; God alone, who sustains the nexus of all our relations and knows us inside out, sees it (Psa 139:23; 1 Cor 13:14).[4] He holds each of our identities secure within his own heart. The Father secures and sustains the promise of access to himself through faith, thereby showing himself to be our Father in whom we may fully trust and rest.

CHAPTER 10

Joyful Mission

There was a man who had two sons. And the younger of them said to his father, "Father, give me the share of property that is coming to me." And he divided his property between them. Not many days later, the younger son gathered all he had and took a journey into a far country, and there he squandered his property in reckless living. And when he had spent everything, a severe famine arose in that country, and he began to be in need. So he went and hired himself out to one of the citizens of that country, who sent him into his fields to feed pigs. And he was longing to be fed with the pods that the pigs ate, and no one gave him anything. But when he came to himself, he said, "How many of my father's hired servants have more than enough bread, but I perish here with hunger! I will arise and go to my father, and I will say to him, 'Father, I have sinned against heaven and before you. I am no longer worthy to be called your son.

Treat me as one of your hired servants.' " And he arose and came to his father. But while he was still a long way off, his father saw him and felt compassion, and ran and embraced him and kissed him. And the son said to him, "Father, I have sinned against heaven and before you. I am no longer worthy to be called your son." But the father said to his servants, "Bring quickly the best robe, and put it on him, and put a ring on his hand, and shoes on his feet. And bring the fattened calf and kill it, and let us eat and celebrate. For this my son was dead, and is alive again; he was lost, and is found." And they began to celebrate.

Now his older son was in the field, and as he came and drew near to the house, he heard music and dancing. And he called one of the servants and asked what these things meant. And he said to him, "Your brother has come, and your father has killed the fattened calf, because he has received him back safe and sound." But he was angry and refused to go in. His father came out and entreated him, but he answered his father, "Look, these many years I have served you, and I never disobeyed your command, yet you never gave me a young goat, that I might celebrate with my friends. But when this son of yours came, who has devoured your property with prostitutes; you killed the fattened calf for him!" And he said to him, "Son, you are always with me, and all that is mine is yours. It was fitting to celebrate and be glad, for this your brother was dead, and is alive; he was lost, and is found" (Luke 15:11–31).

I f we've come into the Lord's family from a troubled background we might identify with the younger son in this parable. If we've grown up within the church we might feel sorry for the older brother who seems to have done everything right but has to watch his younger brother get all the attention. Yet considering the context of the parable steers us away from such a dichotomy. For it isn't about the "good" older brother and the "bad" younger brother at all.

Although usually called "the parable of the Prodigal *Son*," it's more accurate to see it as "the parable of the Lost *Sons*." Both sons were lost; their "lost-ness" is merely expressed differently. The younger brother's rebellion was conspicuous, the elder brother's concealed. The younger son's hatred was revealed in his insolence, the elder son's in self-righteousness. Neither loved their father. The parable uses the brothers to expose *our* distorted views of God, for their sin—like ours—is utterly irrational.

Since we get leverage by condemning others for not meeting our standards, Jesus' mission—to save the world rather than condemn it (John 3:17)—wasn't popular. Despised for keeping company with sinners, Jesus used this parable of the Lost Sons as well as those which preceded it—the parables of the Lost Sheep and the Lost Coin—to explain and defend his mission. He joyfully received and feasted with sinners (Luke 15:1-3) *because this is how the heart of the eternal Father* receives his wayward children; he had been sent into the world to bring God's family home, "to seek and to save the lost" (Luke 19:10).

The joy of being found is the thread uniting this trilogy of parables, each of them unfolding with increasing drama. In the first, the shepherd recovers his lost sheep and invited his friends to join his celebration (Luke 15:5-6). So also the woman, in finding her lost coin (of greater value than the lost sheep) rejoices exuberantly, gathering friends and neighbors in merriment (Luke 15:9). And in the final parable the waiting father implores the elder brother to join the festivities (Luke 15:31-32)—the lavishness of the feast reflecting the priceless value of a son returned. As the climactic parable of the chapter, heaven itself is described where there is "more joy ... over one sinner who repents than over ninety-nine righteous persons who need no repentance" (Luke 15:7).

Though his ministry was primarily directed towards the house of Israel, Jesus knew the Father was gathering the scattered children "from every tribe and language and people and nation" (Rev 5:9; cf. John 11:52), making those who were not a people into a people (Hos 2:23; cf. 1 Pet 2:10). Perhaps the parable refers to this, with the lost Gentile nations represented by the younger brother, and the equally lost but "nearer" Jewish people by the elder. Jesus' gospel comes to both, to those who are far off and those who are near, that *all* might come home with joy (Eph 2:11–17).

But before we continue, consider what the word "prodigal" means. Since the focus has been historically on the "bad" son, we assume prodigal indicates merely wastefulness. This is a legitimate, although narrow, option; and indeed the runaway son was profligate in his expenditure. But the word "prodigal," according to *Merriam-Webster's Collegiate Dictionary*, can also mean "recklessly spendthrift." By this measure *the Father* is the prodigal; he spends lavishly until he has nothing left.

Absolutely Scandalous

The story is culturally scandalous.[1] The appalling actions of the younger son were unimaginable in Jesus' day. Sadly we are too familiar with children telling their parents to get lost (or worse!), but such insolence was unthinkable in the ancient world, particularly amongst rural Jewish families. The son was saying to his father in effect, "I couldn't care less if you were dead. In fact I wish you were—then I'd get out of here and have a good time with my inheritance. Give it to me now!" We cringe at the pain of a loving father attacked in this way.

But to Jesus' audience, the father's response was absolutely scandalous. He didn't erupt with anger, as might have been expected. He let him go peaceably, giving him what he asked, letting him reap the whirlwind he'd sown. This is the way the wrath of God works—giving us over to our sinful choices (see Rom 1:24, 26, 28) that we might cry out to him for mercy: "I will return again to my place, until they acknowledge their guilt and seek my face, and in their distress earnestly seek me" (Hos 5:15). Both sons were given over to their selfish desires, but with different outcomes.

The runaway is given over by his father's prodigal generosity with words like: "Your hatred of me is so great you can't bear to see my face. So, I'll give you up, let you go. You won't think of me; I'll be dead to you. Take what you will if you think it'll help. But regardless, you'll always be my beloved son. My love for you will never be turned back."

The father's reaction is still shocking today. Over the years we've met many whose children went off the rails in early adulthood. Christian counselors frequently advise such parents to set firm boundaries to ensure the wayward leaves home until repentance is evident and then to guardedly receive them back. We've come to believe we must let folk suffer their sin's consequences as imposed by us, that our shunning them is the upshot of their folly. And of course there's the matter of reputation. How would it look if a church leader couldn't discipline his son? Are we to be encouraging ungodly behavior? After all, there has to be some limits to love—tough love. The prodigal son virtually bankrupted the father, let alone his reputation. Yet the father let it happen, without recrimination.

It's common to see God as a larger version of our earthly parents. But even if we've had a positive experience with our parents, we know their limits. Push too far and see what happens. God, however, isn't like *a* father, he's *the* only true Father. His love flows from his unchanging nature, not from our reciprocation of his affection. And so the father in this parable represents God's heart. Where the expectation would be to sever the relationship, the father's actions are dissimilar, so much so his dignity seems overshadowed by the prodigality of his love in letting his son go and more so in receiving him back.

Another scandalous element is the younger brother's return. His reasons are self-centered—hunger, bankruptcy, exposure—so he comes prepared to beg to gain the least possible. Nothing spiritual there. He's as wretched as when he went off, still unable to see his father's heart rightly. He's blown it as a son, and now affixes his hopes on servitude.

While we are told the son "came to himself" in the pigpen (Luke 15:17)—he recognized his sin was against God, and that he'd behaved shamefully before his father—he imagined he was returning to someone like himself. He framed his penitential rhetoric to appeal to his own mindset. Little doubt is left that his welcome was rooted in his father's heart of love rather than any inherent goodness on the son's part. It is indeed the goodness and kindness *of God* that leads to repentance (Rom 2:4) rather than any goodness or kindness in us. Repentance and restoration has always been the aim of our heavenly Father. Thankfully, his ways aren't like ours: His patience doesn't grow thin, and his love is never self-protective.

There is one final, and fairly hidden, scandal to this parable. Undoubtedly a number of Pharisees—the spiritual "elder brothers" of the community—stood among Jesus' audience. Many worked hard to obey the law and had grown contemptuous of the sinners and tax collectors, resenting Jesus' fraternizing with those who were clearly lost. What would become of the nation if a blind eye was turned to the law?

The elder brother has lingered, brooding silently in the background, a silence which speaks loudly of his lack of love for his brother *and his father*. Perhaps we applaud his silence, restraint, and sensible reserve. He is in the right, for he's righteous—or is he? His ire is aroused when he sees his father rejoicing over his brother's return, breaking his silence with complaint. He's indignant with righteous anger and thinks the father should be also. To him the father should scorned the irresponsibility, insolence, and offensiveness of his brother, who was too far on the wrong side of the law for there to be any way home.

This lack of compassion and tenderness just so happens to have cultural ramifications. In ancient Israel, God made provision for a blood relative to act as a redeemer for other members of the extended family in case they fell into debt or slavery. The most well-known Old Testament example of a *go'el* ("kinsman-redeemer") is Boaz, whose actions bought his beloved Ruth from indentured servitude into freedom—and ultimately into marriage. As in their story, the *go'el* had to be a blood relative of the one in need, had to be free (a slave couldn't redeem a slave), had to be willing to act in the capacity, and had to have the resources to pay the redemption price.

For Jesus' hearers, a question would arise: Who is the story's *go'el*? Culturally it should have been the elder brother, but he was hardened against his brother, unwilling to act. Who would redeem the lost if the "righteous" wouldn't go? This dilemma might have led the audience to ask a personal question: "Where's *our go'el*? Will there be a redeemer for us?"

The answer lay in the very person speaking. Jesus himself is our blood relative, and the only one not in need of redemption. He wasn't only willing to come, but rejoiced to do so, bringing with him the redemption price: his life given as a ransom for many (Mark 10:45). Since his heart was one with his Father's, Jesus' desire to bring his lost brothers and sisters home was undeterred, even by the valley of unimaginable darkness posed by the cross.

Scandalous Joy

The runaway recalled the abundance of home, where even the hired servants had food, drink, and shelter (Luke 15:17). But the reception he received, slinking back in guilt, left him astonished rather than abased: his father racing through the village, tunic hiked up to his knees—shameful behavior for a patriarch—embracing him without a word of rebuke or query into the depth of his repentance. He clothed him with *his* best robe, placed a signet ring of power and authority on his finger, and sandals on his feet (a sign of respect, entitling welcomed access across the estate).

Everything within us struggles against this affront to common sense, decency, and order. The extravagance offends us. We've watched loved ones run into the far country unaware and unconcerned with the grief they've caused. Or we've discovered ourselves in the place of the brothers. The parable's conflicting emotions—loss, grief, anger, shame, guilt, despair, and loneliness—aren't foreign. So, isn't "tough love," open repentance, and recompense the answer? Wouldn't disapproving frowns and posting sentries at the gates represent God rightly? Doesn't he demand sensibleness, sobriety, and discipline? And isn't that exactly how we've lived? Yet the truth be known here, with such inclination, *we are* the elder brother—self-righteous, judgmental, and lacking in our view of the Father's abundant love—as well as the younger brother—inflicting pain through selfishness.

But in spite of this, there's no greater joy than coming to the end of ourselves, weeping over our foolishness, and discovering that God doesn't leave us hungry and naked and exposed—he repeatedly runs with joy to cover our shame as we turn homeward. Neither the conscience afflicted by guilt—nor the heart made impervious to grace by self-assuredness believes this. Yet security and peace lie completely outside us. When your conscience is stricken and filled with shame, that is the very time "to turn your eyes away from Law, from works, from your own feelings and conscience, to lay hold upon the gospel and to depend solely on the promise of God ... and the promise produces the sigh that cries: 'Father!' "[2]

If we bolster our conscience with Bible verses and think of our own righteousness, we'll never see the Father's prodigal heart. Reception of the rebel who's wounded us reflects our belief regarding God's receiving of us. Often we may find ourselves fuming: "He doesn't deserve forgiveness!" Yet, by contrast, Luther encourages, "If you see some brother in terror because of a sin of which he has been guilty, run to him, and extend your hand to him in his fallen state. Comfort him with sweet words, and embrace him in your motherly arms."[3] The Father's mercy isn't deserved, yet the flood tide of his goodness flows unstopped to all his wayward children.

The True Son

There are many children but only one true Son. Christ is the only righteous one. The only one who has loved God with all his heart, mind, and strength. He's the only one who shares fully in his Father's joy and can say, "Whoever has seen me has seen the Father" (John 14:9). The mutual love of the Father and Son is oriented wholly away from self and towards the other. This is what unites them in a perfect and self-emptying oneness—utterly complete orientation towards the other. Hence in Jesus we come face to face with the glory of the Father's love, which shines into our self-protective, hard hearts (2 Cor 4:6).

Israel, God's adopted son, was the unceasing object of the Father's care. Hosea's plaintive cry picks this up: "When Israel was a child I loved him, and out of Egypt I called my son" (Hos 11:1). He was born God's son by gracious election and powerful redemption, but sadly Israel comprehensively failed as a son. The northern kingdom of Israel was itself the runway brother, the southern kingdom of Judah, the elder brother. Israel's antics were so appalling that it fell captive to the Assyrians in 722 BC, while Judah scornfully looked on, enjoying self-satisfying prosperity until the Babylonians invaded in 586 BC.

When Jesus came to the lost sheep of Israel, he didn't merely come to (self-) righteous Judah. He also went to Israel, who engaged in pagan worship. Jesus the *Galilean*—whose ministry was as much to the lost tribes of the north as to the Judean remnant in the south—sought the lost where they were. He was the *go'el*, sent to redeem even while he was rejected.

Israel and Judah were failed expressions of sonship, two poles represented by the two brothers. While Israel ran into the far country and joined the pagans, Judah wedded himself to his righteousness so convinced he was *the* defender of God's truth he barely resembled a son at all. The younger brother hoped to return as a mere servant, but was reinstated to full sonship. The elder brother, though fully a son, lived as though he were an orphaned servant. Both misconstrued the Father's heart.

Amazingly, the Father sent his Son to seek them both. We often ridicule the Pharisees, thinking that others fall into their lot but not ourselves. But the parable of the Lost Sons not only exposes the irony of such a response, it emphasizes Jesus' love for the self-righteous Pharisees as much as the self-confessed sinners and tax collectors. The father pleads with the elder brother to share the fullness of his joy, his heart longing for him to return home as his younger brother had.

The Apostle Paul, a Pharisee of Pharisees, testified to how "the grace of our Lord overflowed for [him] with the faith and love that are in Christ Jesus" (1 Tim 1:14). The repentance of either brother would have given equal joy to Jesus, for there aren't two wilfull groups—sinners and Pharisees—but only sinners. He came not to call the righteous but to dine with sinners. The most gracious host sat holy and incognito, exuding inviting love, peace, and joy, in contrast to his austere and exacting hosts (Luke 5:29–32).

It's essential to see the connection between holiness and joy inherent in the Father's calling. God's holiness isn't a passive and stoic flawlessness but an activeness in which he makes certain no separation exists between him and his beloved. When our hearts are touched by such holy love, shame is dissolved and joy is discovered. Those of great joy and substance aren't smug, secure in their own righteousness. Rather, they are those who've experienced the Father's love and forgiveness. They see the depth of their own sin and the greater depth of the Father's inviting holiness. Jesus said, "He who is forgiven little, loves little" (Luke 7:47).

When Jesus ate with the tax collectors and sinners his desire wasn't to be somewhere more holy. He brought with him all the holiness needed to bring his brothers and sisters home, his heart joyfully drinking from the Father's delight as they turn home again (Psa 110:7).

This may prompt the questions: Why doesn't the father in the parable go and find his son? Doesn't he care enough? Such questions are possible only if we've forgotten *who* was telling the parable. Jesus himself is the Father's active response to Israel's failed sonship; in him alone the fullness of the Godhead dwells in bodily form. He is the Father's Word that became flesh. In Jesus, the Father is actively seeking, giving everything he has—his only begotten Son—to bring home his wayward children.

This fact also places the elder brother's complaint in a new context. When he bemoans that a goat has never been sacrificed for him, let alone a fattened calf, he's entirely missed the *Lamb* standing before him. And it's the Father who sent him, willing to number him with the transgressors to redeem the lost.

A Prodigal Woman

Recall the story of Jesus and the Samaritan woman by the well (John 4:1-45). She had had five husbands and was living with yet another man. The community shunned her, so she went at midday when the sun was high to draw from the well alone. What is more, she was without hope of redemption, for she lay outside of Israel, cut off from the temple sacrifices. We could say that all her wells were dry.

She certainly had no hope of coming across the Messiah. But Jesus found her and engaged her with love and compassion, turning her towards the Father with forgiveness. When Jesus told her about her own story the following dialogue ensued:

> "Sir, I perceive that you are a prophet. Our fathers worshiped on this mountain, but you say that in Jerusalem is the place where people ought to worship." Jesus said to her, "Woman, believe me, the hour is coming when neither on this mountain nor in Jerusalem will you worship the Father. You worship what you do not know; we worship what we know, for salvation is from the Jews. But the hour is coming, and is now here, when the true worshipers will worship the Father in spirit and truth, for the Father is seeking such people to worship him (John 4:19-23).

Jesus' statements described what he saw at that very moment. In that encounter—where only Jesus could concurrently reveal and heal her sin—the Father himself was seeking her. There at the well she was being turned to worship the Father through seeing the Son. She had come for a drink in sweltering heat, but discovered a river through a man who touched her lost, empty, ostracized, and wounded soul.

Do you find it at times difficult to believe the Father rejoices over you? Hear again, then, and believe the promise, spoken through Zephaniah:

> The Lord has taken away the judgments against you;
>   he has cleared away your enemies. ...
> The Lord your God is in your midst,
>   a mighty one who will save;
> he will rejoice over you with gladness;
>   he will quiet you by his love;
> he will exult over you with loud singing (Zeph 3:15, 17).

This is the way the Father keeps coming to us. Our joy to be found is matched only by his joyful mission.

CHAPTER 11

Perfecting Sons and Daughters

And have you forgotten the exhortation that addresses you as sons?

> "My son, do not regard lightly the discipline of the Lord,
>   nor be weary when reproved by him.
> For the Lord disciplines the one he loves,
>   and chastises every son whom he receives."

It is for discipline that you have to endure. God is treating you as sons. For what son is there whom his father does not discipline? If you are left without discipline, in which all have participated, then you are illegitimate children and not sons. Besides this, we have had earthly fathers who disciplined us and we respected them. Shall we not much more be subject to the Father of spirits and live? For they disciplined us for a short time as it seemed best to them, but he disciplines us for our good, that we may share his holiness. For the moment all dis-

cipline seems painful rather than pleasant, but later it
yields the peaceful fruit of righteousness to those who
have been trained by it.

Therefore lift your drooping hands and strength-
en your weak knees, and make straight paths for your
feet, so that what is lame may not be put out of joint but
rather be healed (Heb 12:5–13).

A remarkable hand-carved elephant sits on my (Noel's) study
windowsill, reminding me of ministry with a friend and his
countrymen in Andhra Pradesh. It's a treasure not only because
of its fine and accurate detail, but because it is carved from a single piece of solid wood and is hollow!

Its flanks are drilled with intricate holes forming the pattern
of an ornate saddle blanket. But while hollow, it's not empty.
Its maker carved away the interior, leaving a smaller copy of the
elephant inside. And, perhaps as whimsy, the smaller elephant
is facing backwards. Yet, it is always carried forward by the larger elephant.

God is similarly our refuge and hiding place, "a very present
help in time of trouble," says the psalmist (Psa 46:1). We face this
world from *within* the Father; the Church is "*in* God the Father
and the Lord Jesus Christ" (1 Thess 1:1, cf. Acts 17:28). He is, therefore, no absent father. Although we periodically face the wrong
direction, the Father is carrying us to the goal he has for us:
transformation into the perfect image of his Son (2 Cor 3:18).

As he carries us through this life, we're not shielded from pain
and hardship. Persecution, physical afflictions, bereavement and
grief, as well as the turbulence of war, financial crises, relational
difficulties, and natural disasters trouble God's children as much
as they do unbelievers. But so often we misread our suffering
and draw erroneous conclusions about what it means and from
whence it comes.

It's a grave mistake, for example, to stand with Job's comforters, simply attributing suffering to our sin. With different

voices his friends harmonized around one mournful accusation: "You're suffering because you're hiding sin in your heart, in spite of your virtue. If only you'd come clean, confess your sin, God would gladly lift your burden."

Although he was far from clear about what lay behind his suffering, Job had better theology than his friends. As he sat in ashes mourning his loss, he was confident it had *nothing* to do with unconfessed sin. And while neither he nor his comforters saw the whole picture, Job knew God, and he trusted—even in the face of relentless and unbending logic—that his justifying faith would be vindicated.

But blaming the sufferer isn't our only error. We can also err by attributing everything painful or unpleasant to the devil, thereby identifying God's will only with prosperity and comfort.

Undoubtedly Satan stirs the pot vigorously; he has plenty of raw material to work with—hatred, greed and self-interest are close to the hearts of us all. And he has a special vengeance fixed on the sons and daughters of God. Nevertheless, he is a creature—a fallen angel—of limited power and potential. And he too is used by God for our good, in spite of his own intentions.

While Satan might seek to destroy us and our sin may confound us, God's purpose is our perfection. To this end all circumstances transform us so that we might bear his image. Hardships come, but they're never random or pointless. A loving purpose lies beneath them all.

This transforming love doesn't obliterate us. We are distinctive in appearance, personality, calling, and gifts, and our distinctiveness will be preserved for eternity. Yet when the kingdom of Christ has fully come we will all bear his image, his sinless character; that is, we'll trust the Father completely and unreservedly. This is the end to which we're moving as the Church. And such perfection doesn't occur at the expense of our brothers and sisters but as one with them. As God is working through suffering to turn our hearts, souls, minds, and strength to himself, he's also turning us towards each other in love (Luke 10:27). In the end, the whole Church—as an organic whole, not merely as a collection of individuals—shall be shaped to be his dwelling place.

Suffering, therefore, does not contradict divine love. Nor does it grant us leave to self-defensively spite our brothers or sisters either for their suffering or the lack of it. Rather, suffering will have its perfect end in us, as it did in Christ who gave himself up for us, completely trusting the Father (Eph 5:2).

The Perfection of a Son

This perfecting function of suffering is touched upon in the fifth chapter of Hebrews, which says of Jesus:

> Although he was a son, he learned obedience through what he suffered. And being made perfect, he became the source of eternal salvation to all who obey him being designated by God a high priest after the order of Melchizedek (Heb 5:8–10).

Two questions arise from these verses. Is disobedience corrected by suffering? Experience with raising our children would suggest otherwise. Children don't mature merely because they are spanked or scolded; in fact, such means of discipline often result in greater deviance and inculcates neuroses stemming from resentment, self-righteousness, bitterness, and anger. So suffering doesn't necessarily correct disobedience. Why not? Because it doesn't of itself transform the heart, where the root of disobedience resides.

The second question more precisely addresses Jesus. How could suffering perfect Jesus in whom no sin was found? Since suffering isn't an automatic corrective to disobedience, and since Jesus always delighted to do his Father's will, it simply could not perfect him in this way. Therefore, his being made perfect through suffering must mean something else.

In explaining that he was perfected as our high priest, Hebrews 5:9 clues us into the sense in which he was "made perfect" through suffering. His trials and tribulations were the ground on which his faith and obedience were proven. As he encountered hunger and thirst, joy and sorrow, pain and rejection, fatigue and refreshment, he entered into fellowship with our life, joining our battle of faith to entrust ourselves to the Father. Without experiencing the depths of our humanity in this way, he wouldn't have been fit to be our high priest.

In the midst of difficulties, therefore, Jesus grasped firmly onto his Father's promises. His appetite for the Father was stronger than his appetite for a pain-free existence, and this carried him to the cross. In the face of abandonment he looked beyond the cross, trusting the Father to fulfill his promises. It's as though he said, "When I see the dullness and deadness of my disciples' hearts, I recall you've promised a multitude. When I hear the jeers of the crowds, I trust you are with me. When I go through the valley of the shadow of death, still I cry to you, 'Abba! Father!' "

The Perfection of Divine Discipline

The work of the cross is multifaceted, but one of its main aims was to remove a chief barrier to our trusting God by removing the fear of his punishment (1 John 4:18). Where a heart is unsure of forgiveness, or where the conscience is convinced that a particular sin is beyond love's reach, faith yields to fear. Fear and faith are mutually contradictory, and God's purpose is that faith be perfected in love. But we are *not* speaking of faith in our faith. The perfection of faith is the perfection of trust in its object; hence, God's resolute purpose is to cause us to look to and live from our identity in Christ.

Throughout the New Testament we're told that our identity is in Christ. This is a gift of pure grace, received by faith, but not created by faith; it arises from God's work on our behalf. Paul says that we have died and our life is hidden with Christ in God (Col 3:3), that we are seated with Christ in the heavenly places, and that in him God has blessed us with every spiritual blessing (Eph 1:3; 2:6). If this is true, why is it so far from the experience of many?

It is often outside our experience because we're engaged in the very real battle to believe that it is true. This is the foremost struggle of the Christian life. So how is discipline related?

Divine discipline isn't meant to herd us to where we're not, but to confirm where we are. That is, it's aimed at showing us who we truly are in Christ and bringing his life out through us. When faith cleaves to its true identity, a son or daughter finds him or herself under the control of the Holy Spirit and desires to do God's will *from the heart*. This could never have happened beforehand, for there was no passion in the heart to trust God above all else. As a result, love, joy, peace, patience, kindness, goodness, faithfulness, gentleness, and self-control emerge from our lives (Gal 5:22–23)—Christ living through us. Thomas Chalmers says that an "over-mastering positive passion" is the only thing able to actually push out our idolatrous passions for the flesh, i.e., for self, for control, for personal definition of right and wrong, and for performance before man and God.[1]

The New Testament names discipline and suffering as two sides of the same coin. So it is wholly appropriate to see that ultimately suffering comes from the hand of our Father precisely because we are his adopted sons and daughters.

Divine discipline, therefore, is different from our experience with our earthly parents, who disciplined us as seemed best to them (Heb 12:9). What "seemed best" often proceeded from their own thinking, upbringing, character, and goals. While not always the case, the discipline of our children can be reactive and centered merely on behavior modification. The unintended consequence of this is confusion between moral development and faith development—morality and faith are not the same thing! For when behavioral conformity is made primary, discipline becomes punishment. It is a quick step from this to the assumption that behavior is what wins or loses God's approval and gains his blessing or punishment.

Such life training and natural thinking causes us to value external behavior over faith—this was exactly the problem with

Job's friends. But divine discipline is utterly different. It is solely concentrated on faith development; behavior is an outcome of faith, not the focus.

The most commendable earthly discipline modifies behavior and shapes us to be responsible citizens. It doesn't, however, regenerate the heart and promote a passion for trusting God because it leaves untouched our passion for self and self-trust—it doesn't touch the heart. At times we may achieve outward conformity, but only God reaches the heart and causes it to trust something other than itself.

Nevertheless, if earthly discipline is of any benefit, then the writer to the Hebrews asks us to consider how much more helpful is divine discipline: "We have had earthly fathers who disciplined us and we respected them. Shall we not much more be subject to the Father of spirits and live?" (Heb 12:9). Divine discipline is perfectly administered to touch the heart of the Father's beloved in accordance with his desire and ability to work all things for their good (Rom 8:28; cf. Gen 50:20).

At times we communicate frustrated surprise at the failure of our children, saying things such as: "I expected better of you! You should be ashamed of yourself. Now, look what you've done!" But God isn't surprised by our sins, nor by the schemes of the devil against us. He has taken everything into account in Jesus. There is no capriciousness or irrationality in the Father, only holy love that cleanses and heals. This is a comforting truth to come back to.

To further explore the good intention of suffering, consider that the New Testament uses two different words when speaking of discipline and punishment.

When John says, "There is no fear in love, but perfect love casts out fear. For fear has to do with punishment (*kolasis*), and whoever fears has not been perfected in love" (1 John 4:18), he is using a rare word. Jesus used *kolasis* ("punishment") as he describes the last judgment, speaking of the separation between the sheep and the goats: "These [the goats, who are not his] will go away into eternal punishment, but the righteous [the sheep, who are his] into eternal life" (Matt 25:46). The word also appears in 2 Peter 2:9: "Then the Lord knows how to rescue the godly from trials, and to keep the unrighteous under punishment (*kolasis*) until the day of judgment." In Matthew and Peter, God's children are revealed over others.

But where the New Testament speaks of God's discipline of his children, the word *paideia* is used. For example, in Ephesians 6:4, we read: "Fathers, do not provoke your children to anger, but bring them up in the discipline (*paideia*) and instruction of the Lord," and 2 Timothy 3:16 says, "All Scripture is breathed out by God and profitable for teaching, for reproof, for correction, and for training (*paideia*) in righteousness." Hebrews also uses this word consistently in speaking of God's dealings with his beloved children (see Heb 12:5, 7–8, 11).

The point is that in disciplining his children through suffering God is not punishing us as a means of retributive judgment. Rather, he is a proactive parent, looking ahead to the outcome, doing all that is necessary to transform his sons and daughters— not merely in an outward behavioral sense, but with regard to internal passions and motivations.

Why does he bother? He does it for love, so that in the end our hearts and lives would reflect his own; then divine discipline reaches its perfect goal. This stands in contrast to earthly discipline, which often leaves us more bitter and suspicious than loving. The perfection of divine discipline is that it results in joy, not regret (Heb 12:11; cf. 2 Cor 7:10), furthering our love for God rather than driving us into the labyrinth of self-justifying fear.

The Perfection of Faith

It's very difficult not to think of God as a larger version of our parents and thereby to project on to him the suspicion, reserve, and fear that derive from our relation with them. The nerve root of this association between God and our parents is cut only by the revelation of the Father in the face of Jesus Christ (2 Cor 4:6).

Jesus removes suspicion and fear and puts an end to strife as he brings us before the Father's face, where we find our peace in God's peace. He's not a frustrated parent; he's not worried about the outcome; and he's not working out his own insecurities on us. His peace is multiplied to us (1 Pet 1:2) along with love and faith (Eph 6:23), and this keeps our hearts and minds in Christ in a way that passes mere human understanding (Phil 4:7).

The great registry of the faithful in the 11th chapter of Hebrews concludes in the next chapter: "*Therefore*, since we are surrounded by so great a cloud of witnesses ... let us run with endurance the race that is set before us, looking to Jesus, the founder and perfecter of our faith" (Heb 12:1-2). The faithful are the "cloud of witnesses" not in terms of spectators but in terms of those who bear active testimony to the reality of faith. (Witnessing here is "giving testimony.") They all matured through suffering, through which they learned to trust God—to attend to his promises more than their failures and the inadequacy of their circumstances. In other words, they were secured by looking away from themselves to the coming Christ, just as we are by looking to the Christ who has come.

Because Jesus was the "once for all" sacrifice (Heb 10:10) that removed sin and established the new covenant, and because the promises given to Abraham have been fulfilled in him, and because he has become our high priest, and because he is seated in authority at the right hand of the Father, we are completely and eternally secure. Neither tribulation nor death can separate us from the love of God in Christ (Rom 8:35). Therefore, as hard as it might often be to understand, even in suffering we are recipients of grace. For through suffering we attend the same school of obedience as did Christ, that we might be coheirs with him, conformed to his image (Rom 8:29).

Yet, even in this school, we're not thrown back on our own resources for graduation. Christ, who himself learned the difficulty of walking by faith, sustains us in loving-faithfulness, interceding for us, and strengthening us by his Spirit to continue in faith. We are saved by his faithfulness, not only in his work on the cross but also by his faithful commitment to us through this life and into eternity.

And as we continue in faith, the fullness of the Spirit is manifested in our lives, showing himself through the increasingly mature fruit he bears through us. This kind of continuation must therefore be understood as utterly different from "club membership." Suffering is a key element in making this distinction. Throughout Jesus' sufferings he continually entrusted himself to God, casting himself upon his faithfulness (1 Pet 2:23). Such an active-trusting response to trials and tribulations is where God is leading (1 Pet 4:19).

P. T. Forsyth wrote a powerfully relevant treatment of this theme:

> What Christ always demanded of those who came to Him was not character, not achievement, but faith, trust ... faith in Himself as God's Grace. It was trust, and trust not in His manner but in His message, His gospel. That was the one demand of God; and to answer it is perfection. ... Christian perfection is the perfection not of conduct, character, or creed, but of faith. It is not a matter of our behaviour before God the Judge, but of our relation to God the Saviour. Whatever lays the first stress on behaviour or achievement; on orthodoxy, theological, moral, or social; on conformity to a system, a church, a moral type, or a code of conduct; on mere sinlessness, blamelessness, propriety, piety, or sanctity of an unearthly type—that is a departure from the Gospel idea of perfection; which is completeness of trust, and the definite self-assignment of faith amid much imperfection.[2]

Most of us are slow of heart to believe this. So wedded are we to the idea of performance-based acceptance, and so prone are we to identify suffering with retributive punishment, we find it difficult to believe for certain that we have a reconciled God, especially when we are in the midst of the fires. Yet even as we pass through them, they do not destroy us, just as the deep waters do not overwhelm us (Isa 43:2), for we pass through them in God the Father and in our Lord Jesus Christ. We are never forsaken, never alone, never abandoned to our own devices, for we are never separated. God lays his hand on us only to bless and heal, always at peace with what he has done and is doing, and utterly sure of the outcome. This, and only this, enables us to embrace suffering, knowing that as we seek the Father's face, our feeble hearts and hands are strengthened by grace, granting us what we need above all else: faith to believe and trust.

CHAPTER 12

The United Family

The more we know God as Father, the more we find our personal identity in Christ, the more functionally united we shall become as a Christian community. Our unity is, therefore, wholly a result of faith until we see our Savior face-to-face.

It's impossible to overstate the importance of unity. Teams, parties, boards, and marriages function poorly without it. It's not surprising, therefore, the amount of time, money, and energy we pour into creating and sustaining unity. Yet the kind of unity sought, as well as the way we seek it, is often saturated with evil. And that's difficult news to accept.

As much as we claim the contrary, we are turned in on ourselves, upon *our* thoughts and desires (Gen 6:5; cf. Matt 24:37). Hence the form of unity we seek typically enslaves rather than emancipates. Tribalism and sectarianism, for example, both demonstrate this. Attempts at "unity in diversity" also fail because of an ever-present pull from consensus to corruption. Self-interest overrides altruism; tolerance becomes inquisition.

Nevertheless, the power of unity, notwithstanding its short shelf life, is self-evident. Adolf Hitler's Third Reich is an extreme example, but it illustrates well the point. Hitler built the Third Reich on unity, with himself its father figure. Hope in the promises of "the father" united and reinvigorated a demoralized nation and economy. And once unity was established, devotion to the Reich was matched only by hatred of those outside it. The father was kind to his family, especially his favored sons, but ruthlessly hostile to foreigners.

Creating such unity was hard work for Hitler, and keeping it required continual reinforcement by fear and love alike. The quasi-religious rallies of Nazi Nuremberg—with cathedrals of light framing massed spectaculars, nationalistic music, and powerful rhetoric—"converted" hundreds of thousands to the cause. Meanwhile, repression, torture, and murder kept boundaries tight, buttressing devotion to the father. The "common enemy" was common only because of a manipulated unity.

Isolation, rejection, and exclusivism have always been the mainstays of our attempts to create and keep unity. Political parties rally followers around charismatic figures while running fear campaigns to discredit opponents. Everywhere unity tends to be a "carrot and stick" creation. The church is no exception: The Crusades, the Spanish Inquisition, and the Salem witch trials are a few infamous examples where the church's means and ends have been colored by the toxins of power and control. The entertainment-driven consumer-mindedness of the contemporary church may seem benign in comparison, but it simply turns power and control over to the appetites of the collective; isolation, rejection, exclusivism merely take on a more subtle form.

The power of unity shouldn't surprise us. We've been created in the image of God, who is One, so we have an inescapable, albeit unconscious, drive for oneness. The tri-unity of God, however, is unlike anything we know or seek to set up. Our notions of unity are intrinsically exclusionary, being founded on ideologies that close down the borders of our lives, patrolling them with force.

Unity and uniformity are thereby conflated, so to speak with a different voice threatens the status quo.

By contrast, God's unity is uncreated and eternal, and, therefore, it is eternally *open*. It embraces the outsider, to the point of self-sacrificial death through the Son. The cross is the Father's flinging open the doors of his house, gathering us as sons and daughters as one family filled with his Spirit. As we are personally touched by this active openness of God, the Church's unity also becomes active and constructive. In other words, the more the Church is focused on God, as opposed to itself, the more openhearted and loving it becomes. The more we are filled with the Holy Spirit, as opposed to self, the more Christ's love overflows through us. Strangers are welcomed and enemies embraced because Jesus' life permeates his body, which the Church is (Col 1:18).

The point of this final chapter is simple: God, who is One, *has made us one*. This is the true context of our lives, and it is a great hope of the world to come. Additionally, it is the very thing Jesus prayed for before his arrest:

> I am praying not only for these disciples but also for all who will ever believe in me through their message. I pray that they will all be one, just as you and I are one— as you are in me, Father, and I am in you. And may they be in us so that the world will believe you sent me.
>
> I have given them the glory you gave me, so they may be one as we are one. I am in them and you are in me. May they experience such perfect unity that the world will know that you sent me and that you love them as much as you love me (John 17:20-23 NLT).

This oneness is a gift touching our souls deeply with transformative love, just as disunity leaves us tattered and torn. Perhaps this is why dissension and division is such an abomination to the Lord (cf. Prov 6:19; Gal 5:20); it's a denial of all that he is and all he's made us to be. God's creation of one family, however, is both a mystery and a confession of faith.

In the New Testament, a mystery is not passive, but an active and transformative reality. Tomas Halik has captured this well:

> One must never consider mystery "over and done with." Mystery, unlike a mere dilemma, cannot be overcome; one must wait patiently at its threshold and persevere in it—must carry it in one's heart—just as Jesus's mother did according to the Gospel, and allow it to mature there and lead one in turn to maturity.[1]

Like all of God's revelation, we receive unity by faith. We *believe* in the holy Christian Church, and the communion of saints (Apostles' Creed).[2] Such unity may not be fully experienced now, but we believe in its current existence and know it to be our assured future hope.

One God, One People

Psalms 120–134 carry the designator, "A Song of Ascents." Scholars suggest these psalms were sung as the people of Israel made their way to Jerusalem to worship during the great pilgrimage feasts. As the various tribes made their way to the temple—journeying from their houses to the house of God—they knew they were one people, united under the one covenant. Their unity wasn't found simply in their common history, but in their common identity as God's beloved people—they were united by his covenant faithfulness.

> Behold, how good and pleasant it is
>   when brothers dwell in unity!
> It is like the precious oil on the head,
>   running down on the beard,
> on the beard of Aaron,
>   running down on the collar of his robes!
> It is like the dew of Hermon,
>   which falls on the mountains of Zion!

For there the Lord has commanded the blessing,
life forevermore (Psa 133).

Psalm 133 celebrates something *only God can effect*: "Behold, how good and pleasant it is when brothers dwell in unity!" (Psa 133:1). Fellowship is a gift. It can't be artificially generated. We've been trying to do that since the Tower of Babel, and the result is always the same—disintegration. The scattering that took place at Babel wasn't due to God feeling threatened by the efforts of the tower builders, but because any "unity" that doesn't have its basis in God is inherently oppressive; mercifully he doesn't allow it to stand for long. In contrast, the psalm pictures the abiding unity of God's family in two ways.

The first picture likens unity to precious oil running down on the beard of Aaron and onto the collar of his robes. What's in view here is the specially perfumed anointing oil that was used exclusively within the temple (see Exod 30:22–38). It was set apart for the Lord's use, thus forming the distinctive fragrance of his house. With it, the utensils, the sanctuary itself, the altars, and the priests were anointed, dedicated by him for his use.

Can you picture Aaron, or one of his descendants, with oil running down from the crown of his head to the hem of his garments? It not only soaked his clothing, but penetrated his pores. Whenever or wherever he moved the aroma surrounded him— indeed it arose from him—setting him apart as a holy gift to serve his brothers.

In a representative sense, he *was* God's gathered people. He stood for them in the temple; and they stood with him before the altar of God. The Holy Spirit's anointing of him was a token of God's presence to the whole of the assembled nation. Yet where the ancient high priests were imperfect and prevented by death from continuing in office, Jesus stands with and for us in the presence of God eternally (Heb 7:17). His aroma is now ours, surrounding us in the Father's presence.

The second picture is geographical: "It is like the dew of Hermon, which falls on the mountains of Zion!" (Psa 133:3).

This is an impossible feat. Mount Hermon lies to the north of the Sea of Galilee near Lebanon, while Mount Zion is the eastern hill of Jerusalem. Albeit an exaggeration, it's akin to saying the snows of Everest fall on Kilimanjaro!

Why use such an impossible picture? Two reasons suggest themselves. It may refer to the unity of the tribes of Israel: North and south were one in God's eyes, even if their history was filled with strife. But the impossible geography may also represent something spiritual. The Creator can do what we can't: heal old scars and reconcile us to him and each other in Jesus.

How does such unity occur? The second half of Psalm 133:3 indicates that unity comes specifically through the divine blessing of life: "For there the Lord has commanded the blessing, life forevermore." In other words, the unity of God's people lies in *his* defeat of death, in his irrevocable blessing in removing the law's curse (Gal 3:13).

Disunity actually results from the fear of death. The imminent end of natural life pressures us to fashion security and significance for ourselves in the immediate present—to provide life for ourselves. And anything that detracts from our security and significance, our personal worth, is taken for an instrument of death, tearing immediate life and liberty from us. Covetousness, theft, and murder, even contemptuous attitudes and judgmental words, are all attempts to give ourselves life. Like orphans abandoned to the city streets, we very often think and act as if this is the only life. Division, envy, competition, jealousy, and bitterness, therefore, arise from a subterranean self-centeredness in which we're desperately grasping for this life, failing to live in the reality of the fullness of life in Jesus alone, "life forevermore." But if we have eternal life in Jesus, will not the Father freely give us *all good things*? Trusting in his constant love through the gospel frees us from self-preserving rivalry, liberating us to love and serve one another generously from the heart.

Christian Community

The unity Israel experienced in its sacred pilgrim feasts was a foretaste of eternity. As the tribes of Israel brought their glory into the temple from the four corners of the promised land, so also will the nations bring their glory into the temple of the triune God (Rev 21:24-26). The events of Pentecost (see Acts 2), therefore, both ended the Old Testament pattern of pilgrimage feasts and heralded the coming great procession.

At Pentecost, Jews from all corners of the known world gathered in Jerusalem. They had come for Passover and stayed an extra 50 days until Pentecost. When the Holy Spirit came upon them, they realized they were recipients of a decisive divine action, sharers in something beyond themselves that embraced them all. Each was saved, but more importantly they were part of a saved *community*. And the love shared among them took their breath away. It was as impossible as the dew of Hermon coming down upon Zion, yet it was more real than anything they had ever known. None of this arose from themselves; it came by the Father's grace, which brought new life through a spiritual resurrection, uniting this now-living community together in the living Christ. As oil had flowed down on Aaron, the Spirit anointed the assembled believers, saturating their mind, emotions, and will—a sign of an impossible gift.

The unity was clearly from above. Drenched by the Spirit with the fragrance of Christ, they became an aroma to the whole world—of life to some and death to others. But regardless of the response, the fragrance of Jesus was upon them. As the Spirit took the gospel to Judea, Samaria, and thence to the whole known world, the same things happened. Disintegrated lives were integrated, cultures were united, Jews, Gentiles, slaves, free, male, and female, all cried out, "Abba! Father!" by the same Spirit.

So, by definition, the Church abides in God and he abides in the Church (cf. 1 John 4:13). As partakers of the same Spirit, believers are members of Christ's body and thereby—and only thereby—members of one another. This means true Christian community is community in and through Christ alone, not through coercion, carrots, or cravings. It might come as a shock, but merely gathering in a church building doesn't constitute Christian community—it can actually be, at times, the farthest thing from Christian community.

In his book *Life Together*, Dietrich Bonhoeffer wrote about community being grounded in Christ alone:

> One is a brother or sister to another only through Jesus Christ. I am a brother or sister to another person through what Jesus Christ has done for me and to me; others have become brothers and sisters to me through what Jesus Christ has done for them and to them. The fact that we are brethren only through Jesus Christ is of immeasurable significance. Therefore, the other who comes face to face with me earnestly and devoutly seeking community is not the brother or sister with whom I am to relate in the community. My brother or sister is instead that other person who has been redeemed by Christ, absolved from sin, and called to faith and eternal life. What persons are in themselves as Christians, in their inwardness and piety, cannot constitute the basis of our community, which is determined by what those persons are in terms of Christ. Our community consists solely in what Christ has done to both of us. That not only is true at the beginning, as if in the course of time something else were to be added to our community, but also remains so for all the future and into all eternity. I have community with others and will continue to have it only through Jesus Christ. The more genuine and the deeper our community becomes, the more everything else between us will recede, and the more clearly and purely will Jesus Christ and his work become the one and only thing that is alive between us. We have one another only through Christ, but through Christ we really do have one another. We have one another completely

and for all eternity. ... It is essential for Christian community that two things become clear right from the beginning. *First, Christian community is not an ideal, but a
divine reality; second, Christian community is a spiritual
[pneumatische] and not a psychic [psychische] reality.*[3]

Christian community, then, is not something to be attained—
an idealistic project—but is already a divine reality experienced
as we relate to each other in Christ. It's not primarily a unity of
head (mental or cognitive; signing up to the same policies and
platforms), although this is not to be ignored. Rather, it's a unity
of heart, a unity in the Spirit characterized by the fruit of the
Spirit: love, joy, peace, patience, kindness, goodness, faithfulness,
gentleness, and self-control (Gal 5:22–23). In Christ, then, we are
united in a worshipful community even to those who may not
share our exact individual theological convictions and to those
who for a time may regard us as their enemy. We are brothers
and sisters to many whose language, culture, and church tradi-
tions are very different from ours, and they are one with each of
us, even if we've never met.

Greater than Conceived

Our unity in Christ is greater than our ability to conceive it.
Yet, paradoxically, both joy and grief testify to it, and both of
these come from the Spirit of God.

On the one hand, we are united to the Father and the Son
by God's love poured into our hearts through the Holy Spirit
(Rom 5:5). Inexpressible joy is experienced as we relate to each
other in the Spirit. In fact, participation together in the love of
God is so renewing, New Testament believers virtually invented
a new vocabulary: *Koinonia* and *agape* are but two of its expressions. The book of Acts tells how the early Christian community
lived: Property was used selflessly; others' needs were preferred
over one's own; widows and the poor were cared for; suffering
was endured with joy; prayers and supplications were offered on

behalf of all, even for one's enemies; and, as the Spirit blew, nations were touched with the good news of the gospel that bound this community together.

On the other hand, the Spirit's presence is always accompanied by grief. In the Spirit, we not only "rejoice with those who rejoice, [but] weep with those who weep" (Rom 12:15). Although unity in Christ is never broken, death, for example, disrupts it. We grieve in direct proportion to the depth of the love which engendered it. While grief in the New Testament is shot through with hope, the pain of separation is real, and we long for the face to face communion with those who have gone before us. But it's not just death that testifies to our essential unity. We feel grief in the loss of relationship, in the dislocation of fellowship, and the loss of affection in the body of Christ. Yet while disagreements cloud it, mistakes and misjudgments stalk it, sin of all kinds bedevils it, and stubbornness of heart seems to defy it, the reality of the unity of Christ's body will be unveiled on the last day. Then we'll come to know each other free from any hint of guilt, shame, reproach, or resentment, filled only with the fruit of the Spirit. "I shall know fully, even as I have been fully known," says Paul (1 Cor 13:12). In other words, the perfect love Jesus has for the Father shall be the same love we have for the Father, the result of which will be that nothing but love shall flow from us.[4]

Even the best of our Christian communities give plenty of opportunity for disagreement; many habits we find personally off-putting, some actions are thoughtless and self-centered, some interpretations of Scripture are held with brutal dogmatism, and the threat of self-righteousness is always present. This is why the more we find our personal identity *in Christ*, the more functionally one our community will become. For he is the only ground and future for our lives together as well as the only ground for true forgiveness and compassion.

2 Corinthians 3:18 puts it this way: "We all, with unveiled face, beholding the glory of the Lord, are being transformed into the same image from one degree of glory to another. For this comes

from the Lord who is the Spirit." Two features of the verse stand out.

First, the subject is plural: *we*. There's no independence or competition for perfection here. Rivalry; boasting over and against one another; the false humility of inverted pride that wallows in self-pity as excuse to evade the Father's love—these and many other expressions of the flesh are ruled out. Hence this focus on the "we" of community is transformative, for it turns us outward together, facing the Son, each one as dependent on his grace as the next.

Second, we—the subject—are passive: We *are being transformed*; we *behold* the Lord. Transformation occurs as our gaze lingers on the face of Jesus turned towards us. Notice that "behold" is radically different from striving to see, as if he were hidden or evasive. Beholding is, rather, basking in the light of his loving and attentive face, resting in his arms, bound up in his blessing. This experience shall reach its perfection come the last day, but its reality may be enjoyed even in the present by faith. For as the Apostle John counseled, "Beloved, we are God's children now, and what we will be has not yet appeared; but we know that when he appears we shall be like him, *because we shall see him as he is*" (1 John 3:2). In beholding him by faith, we are home, even in the turbulence of today.

> One day we'll see Him face to face,
> And then our hearts will beat as one,
> That day we'll know the glory of His grace,
> As we on earth have never known.
>
> The years of sorrow and of strife,
> The sin that brought a holy shame,
> The guilt our hearts could never wholly hide
> Will never visit us again.
>
> Dear Lover, Savior, Jesus Christ,
> Our present life is hid in Thee,

But oh! the wonder when we are unveiled
In glory of our liberty.

Till then we live in present hope,
In patience of the coming sight,
And those who share with You Your glory now,
We then will meet with great delight.[5]

Conclusion

We live always by the Father's grace whether we feel his presence or not, whether our mind and emotions are stable enough to grasp that fact or not. As sons and daughters of the heavenly Father, we have a heavenly home and an eternal hope. God has made us one with the Son and thereby one with all other members of his body, eternally. Christ secures all of this. And yet it is not simply a truth to give assent to, to grasp with the mind, a truth which remains outside of us. The Spirit of the Father even now causes us to long for the inheritance which awaits us and "front ends" it into our souls in the present, which in biblical terms is called "the first-fruits of the Spirit" (Rom 8:23). Conflict and suffering, joy and triumph; each alike prepares us for what we are yet to be and to see, yet each in its own way testifies to the gift of the unity which has been given to us from above.

When all is said and done, God has said all and done all. None of us will stand before him in heaven, boasting of what a good job we did, how *we* arrived. When we see him face to face there will be no room for such self-vaunting piety. Instead we'll see the oneness of the Father, Son, and Spirit in the very lives of those with whom we stand. Each will love, honor, glorify, and serve the other as Christ has us. And the whole multitude, with one voice, will cry, "Abba! Father!" That is the glory to which we are called; it will be the fullness of sonship fully revealed.

And the glory of his grace lies in this: The Father has planned it so; he has given his Son that it may be so; and he has poured out the Spirit as the pledge that it will be so. Even so, come Lord Jesus!

Afterword

We started this book by saying it wasn't for those who have it all together. Now that you've come to the end, you still won't. We, the authors, still don't. More than ever before, we see that the Christian life consists not of a set of theological formulae or pietistic techniques, left in our hands to apply, but trust! Paul's testimony must become ours: "The life I now live in the body, I live by faith in the Son of God, who loved me and gave himself for me" (Gal 2:20 NIV). This book has simply endeavored to unpack this statement from the perspective of the fatherhood of God.

The Son who has loved us faithfully is none other than the Son of the Father. The Spirit poured out through Jesus on the day of Pentecost is none other than the Spirit of the Father. Thus, while we see the Father through the other persons of the Trinity, we see *the Father!* Recall Jesus' reply to Philip, "Whoever has seen me has seen the Father" (John 14:9). So we love the Father, trust the Father, and long for the Father through his Son and Spirit.

The trust, therefore, that marks the Christian life is not trust in "God," undefined and unnamed, but in our Abba whose character we see in the face of Jesus. This is truly miraculous! Such trust doesn't naturally arise from the human heart, least of all when it's filled with pain.

We never come to behold the Father, apart from his work. He planned and purposed our redemption before time. He initiated the covenant promises, revealing them to his ancient people. He attended Israel's infant steps, preparing its history as a seed bed for the coming Son. And when the time had fully come, he sent the Son to seek and save us. He redeemed us through the shadow of the cross and the brilliance of the resurrection. He bestowed the gift of the Spirit so we might experience the life-changing presence of the living God, turning shame into praise and rebellion into the obedience of faith. He ordained the end from the beginning, setting the day of the Son's glorious reappearing. And he will not fail to transform us into the image of his Son, that we may be united and filled with his fullness. Our losses, our shame, our sin, our sheer confusion, as also our resurrection to a new life and future—every facet of our story is embraced in this overarching story of Abba's love.

The Father, then, is the one we trust. We live by his Word, take refuge in his promises, and live in the shadow of his wings. The cross is our North Star, because there, *as in no other place,* do we find the greatness of the Father's love. "He who did not spare his own Son but gave him up for us all, how will he not also with him graciously give us all things?" (Rom 8:32). Certainly he has! He has freed us from the curse of the law, and secured us in love.

The world, the flesh, and the devil portray the Father other than he is. We hear their voices of accusation and we ourselves may wrongly project the faults and flaws of our earthly fathers and mothers onto the face of God. But do we not yet see, we are not orphans? We are sons and daughters, the children of hope, in a cynical and despairing hour.

We still traverse valleys of deep darkness. Grief and loss as much as joy and thanksgiving accompany our steps. Our hearts can be overwhelmed by sorrow, our minds clouded by a cacophony of messages. But by grace we learn to trust. Abba draws near with manna enough for today. He leads us by the hand, redirecting our troubled hearts and minds, tenderly whispering the Word of the gospel once more, thereby lifting our face to meet his loving gaze.

We don't know what you are facing, or what you may yet be called to face. But we know you are invited to see God as Father, to know the one who does know, to rest in his bountiful arms, and to be embraced by his expansive heart. Let him do in and through you what he needs. Don't try to unpack and control the mystery this life is. But entrust your ways to him, realizing you are loved, your identity hidden in the Son, your future secured by the triune God.

But let not the last word be ours. Let it be his...

> When the fullness of time had come, God sent forth his Son, born of woman, born under the law, to redeem those who were under the law, so that we might receive adoption as sons. And because you are sons, God has sent the Spirit of his Son into our hearts, crying, "Abba! Father!" So you are no longer a slave, but a son, and if a son, then an heir through God (Gal 4:4-7).

Seize this hope!

Study Guide

by Lee Beckham

Introduction

1. "God knows what we really need, as a good Father should" (*Embracing God as Father*, 1). What other qualities do you think a father should have? Did your father have these qualities?

_____

_____

_____

_____

2. When you hear the word "father," what image comes to mind? What qualities come to mind? Where do these images and qualities come from? What has informed your thinking about fathers and fatherhood?

_____

_____

_____

_____

3. In the Trinity, we see God the Father as the eternal Father in intimate relationship with God the Son and God the Holy Spirit. Does seeing God in this context change the way you view him?

_____

_____

_____

_____

4. In common usage, "hope" is often interchangeable with "wish," representing a desire unfounded on anything concrete. But in the Bible, "hope" represents a solid certainty founded on God's promises. Has the surety of God's promises been important to your thinking of God as your father? "Hope deferred makes the heart sick, but a desire fulfilled is a tree of life" (Prov 13:12). After reading this verse, what effect should the knowledge of our true hope have on us?

_____

_____

_____

_____

_____

5. Have you ever considered how a father may need to use "troubles" in the life of his child? When my daughter was only a few days old, my wife and I took her for her first doctor's visit. At the end of it, she had to have a shot. Even knowing how important the immunization was for her health and well-being, it was extremely hard for me to subject her to it and to watch her reaction to the pain of it. Does this story change your answer to the original question?

_____

_____

_____

_____

_____

6. Many Christians find it very natural to see a connection between their behavior and God's disposition towards them. For instance, when I was in college, I felt anxious going into an examination if I had not had my usual morning devotional time. All my Christian friends felt the same way. Have you ever felt that God would "be out to get you" over some failing?

_____

_____

_____

7. The desire to pay some price for their failings or to make some contribution toward earning their salvation is common among Christians. Have you ever felt that?

_____

_____

_____

_____

Now read this quote from Thomas Chalmers: "Along with the light of a free Gospel, does there enter the love of the Gospel, which, in proportion as we impair the freeness, we are sure to chase away." Do you see how drastic an effect that desire can have? "We're subject to a restless conscience and to the suspicion that God isn't *for* us unless we earn his favor and keep ourselves in it" (*Embracing God as Father*, 8).

Contrast that attitude with more of Chalmers: "And never does the sinner find within himself so mighty a moral transformation, as when under the belief that he is saved by grace, he feels constrained thereby to offer his heart a devoted thing, and to deny ungodliness."[1]

Have you experienced the transforming power that results from seeing that God saved you because he loved you—despite your undeserving status?

_____

_____

_____

_____

Chapter 1—God the Father: All in All

1. How do you enjoy God? Have you ever thought of your relationship with God in those terms?

_____

_____

_____

_____

2. Paul describes the end of human history as the fulfillment of the Father's plan. Have you ever thought about eternity in that way? Do you think about your own life in the same way—as the fulfillment of the Father's plan for you? How does that make you feel about your life?

_____

_____

_____

_____

3. "The knowledge of God as Father has been lost through sin, corruption, and rebellion (Rom 1:18-32) with the result that we've turned in on ourselves, seeking to meet our own desires at the expense of others" (*Embracing God as Father*, 14). Does this seem an extreme statement to you? How much impact on your life do you expect furthering your understanding of God as your Father to have?

_____

_____

_____

4. "The world thinks it defines itself—that it gives itself mean-ing, hope, and security. As it goes about defining, making, and se-curing itself, it's actually about the business of destroying itself" (*Embracing God as Father*, 14–15). What things do you see the world today trying to define for itself? What consequences do you see from this?

_____

_____

_____

5. "God's promises have always anticipated deliverance from all that's blocked us from knowing ourselves as the object of the Father's affection—the blockage is the sin of our own hard hearts" (*Embracing God as Father*, 16). How has your sin kept you from knowing God as your Father? Do you think you have begun to understand how deep and pervasive your sin is?

_____

_____

_____

6. Seeing God and ourselves rightly has often been described as a key part of the Christian life. Seeing God clearly has been a shattering experience for some (see Isa 6). Some truths are so difficult, we must comprehend them over time. Do you think you see God rightly? What about yourself? Do you embrace what the Bible tells you about yourself?

_____

_____

_____

_____

7. "Just as we have borne the image of the man of dust, we shall also bear the image of the man of heaven" (1 Cor 15:49). Do you ever feel that you are a "man of dust"? Does it thrill your heart to read those words and know that you will be a "man of heaven"?

_____

_____

_____

_____

Chapter 2—Filled with Fullness

1. In what ways have you seen the firstfruits principle in your own life?

_____

_____

_____

_____

2. "The quality of *our* resurrected life is thereby guaranteed by virtue of *his*" (*Embracing God as Father*, 23). How often do you think about your resurrected life? What do you think it will be like?

_____

_____

_____

_____

3. The verses of 1 Corinthians 15:20–24, quoted in this chapter, were set to music by George F. Handel in his *Messiah*. Find a copy and listen to it while meditating on these verses. ("I know that my Redeemer liveth" and "Since by man came death" are the parts with the verses from 1 Corinthians 15 and can be found easily online.)

_____

_____

_____

_____

4. "Christ comes to us not with closed fists and crossed arms. No, his hands and arms are flung wide open revealing his own open heart" (*Embracing God as Father*, 29). How often do you think of Jesus being open to you? Commit to keeping this precious image in your mind. When you go to pray today, stop and think of Christ standing with arms wide open to you.

_____

_____

_____

5. "Jesus has been given as head over all things *to the Church*" (*Embracing God as Father*, 26). The idea of Jesus as head of the Church is common for Christians, but how does the idea of God giving Jesus to the church to be the head affect your feelings about this?

_____

_____

_____

_____

6. "[A]ll of the world's happenings ... occur for the good of the Church" (*Embracing God as Father*, 26). This is not an easy statement to swallow. What events do you struggle to see as being for the good of the church? Is it hard to trust in God's sovereign provision for his Church?

_____

_____

_____

_____

7. "[W]hat God is able to do, and is doing, is far more abundant 'than all that we ask or think' (Eph 3:20)" (*Embracing God as Father*, 28). Take a moment to recall a time in your life when God did far more than you asked or thought. How has God's goodness affected your willingness to give?

_____

_____

8. "All our lives we've been taught you don't get something for nothing, and what you earn is in accordance with how hard you work" (*Embracing God as Father*, 29). How hard is it for you to believe that God wants to bless you even when you have failed?

_____

_____

9. "But in the time of tribulation I will not listen to or accept Christ except as a gift" (Luther, quoted in *Embracing God as Father*).[1] Take some time to reflect on God's gift of Christ to you, not as an example to strive after, but as a savior to provide a way for you to join God's family.

_____

_____

10. Will you be content with your thimble, or do you want to experience the ocean? How will your life be different if you give up "twisting God's arm" with good works and instead believe and trust that all the fullness of God is already yours?

_____

_____

_____

Chapter 3—The Father's Plan

1. Two pastors went out to enjoy a round of golf on their day off. The first pastor's drive on the first hole went down the fairway, veered well to the right, then bounced on a paved cart path before ricocheting off a tree back onto the fairway and rolling to a stop a good 40 yards further than his average drive. After a few seconds of bemused silence, the pastor turned to his friend and said, "Did I tell you what a great quiet time I had this morning?" They had a good laugh. The second pastor later used this as an illustration to show the tendencies of our hearts. The joke assumes that even though God is in control of the details of our lives, he only works things out well for us (or to our liking) when we have done something to earn it. How common do you think this belief is?

_____

_____

_____

_____

2. How often do you think about how responding to the gospel should look in your life? Has the gospel become for you, like Luther, "a gateway into heaven"?[1]

_____

_____

_____

_____

_____

3. "Too readily we decide for ourselves or others what 'bless-ing' should look like, and too readily assume that suffering and adversity are signs of God's curse" (*Embracing God as Father*, 40). Can you recall a time when you felt you were under God's curse, but later it became apparent he was blessing you? How does that experience affect your outlook on the circumstances of your life?

_____

_____

_____

4. "Our deeply ingrained work ethic causes us to view everything God does in utilitarian terms. If God does something, it must be because he wants us to do something in return" (*Embracing God as Father*, 42). How often do you find yourself thinking this way? Would it cause you shame to enjoy God's blessings if you felt you had not earned them? Why?

_____

_____

_____

_____

5. As you have journeyed further with God, do you find your-self more drawn to "works of love and mercy, ... justice and joy" (*Embracing God as Father*, 43)?

_____

_____

_____

_____

6. "They didn't earn their redemption by keeping the law. The law was a gift that followed redemption" (*Embracing God as Father*, 43). Do you see the timing here (i.e., the law being given after redemption, not before) as part of God's plan for dealing with his children? Why would God bring the Israelites out of slavery if it wasn't for keeping the law?

_____

_____

_____

_____

7. Look back over the course of your life. Which has been more characteristic of your life: using the law to gain righteousness or letting your failure to keep the law point you to God's promise?

_____

_____

_____

_____

8. Which of the three promises (described in this chapter) is most appealing to you: God remembering your sin no more, having your heart of stone replaced by a heart of flesh, or being clean from your uncleannesses? Why?

_____

_____

_____

_____

9. Do you feel that there is still something to be worked out with your salvation? Is there anything still to be atoned for? How does the offering of the body of Jesus Christ once for all (Heb 10:10) address those feelings?

_____

_____

_____

_____

10. Reread the story, found in this chapter, about phantom pain. Does that remind you of how you still feel the guilt of your sin?

_____

_____

_____

_____

11. Take a moment to remember the last time you looked away from yourself to the Lamb and felt a deep cry for the Father escape from your heart.

_____

_____

_____

_____

Chapter 4—The Lord in Our Midst

1. What does your "persistent rebellion against God" (*Embracing God as Father*, 50) look like? Have you felt that you faced ruin or a type of captivity because of your failures? Do you see that you need to be saved from yourself?

_____

_____

_____

2. As you look over your life, into what area do you think the biggest problems fall?

_____

_____

_____

"Josiah recognized the nation's problems weren't political or economic, but spiritual" (*Embracing God as Father*, 51). Can you accept this verdict about your own life? How has corrupt worship been a part of your problems? What idols have you served?

_____

_____

_____

3. Why do you think it is so hard for God's people to hear the words of true prophets and so easy to listen to false prophets? Can you recall a time when you chose to listen to a message that was easier to hear and later realized your folly?

_____

_____

_____

4. "The Lord's discipline is full of promise, not threat, setting us free to love and be loved" (*Embracing God as Father*, 53). Think back over your life to the times you received discipline (whether from parents, teachers, etc.). Was that discipline full of promise or full of threat? How did you react to it?

_____

_____

_____

5. One of the greatest challenges for God's people is to learn to believe what God has said in his word and not to judge their lives by their external circumstances. Is your assessment of your situation in life swayed more by your physical circumstances or by what you believe about God?

_____

_____

_____

6. "Deliverance for a besieged city or a besieged heart has to come from outside" (*Embracing God as Father*, 54). Have you experienced the futility of trying to help yourself when your heart is besieged?

_____

_____

_____

7. "In saying this, Jesus intimately identifies himself with those sinners coming for baptism" (*Embracing God as Father*, 57). How does this change your understanding of the significance of Jesus' name, Emmanuel ("God with us")?

_____

_____

_____

8. "You remain a slave to sin not because you continue to struggle with it, but because of *the false impression that deeper dedication and effort to obey the law will set you free*" (*Embracing God as Father*, 60). How do you react to this statement? What is your experience with deeper dedication and effort to obey the law? Did it produce the desired results?

_____

_____

_____

9. "A besieged city is cut off from hope and given over to despair. Relief for such a city doesn't come through the recitation of what it *ought* to have done, or the preparations it *should* have made" (*Embracing God as Father*, 60). Much of what passes for words of hope in our churches fit into these last two categories. Why is it so hard to resist saying such things to people (including ourselves) in tough situations?

_____

_____

_____

10. "[I]t's important to emphasize that commandments, commitments, and conduct (i.e., works of the law) cannot avert sin's siege. The law brings no exclamation of delight, because 'the law is not of faith' (Gal 3:12)" (*Embracing God as Father*, 60–61). The human heart is naturally drawn to works of the law as a means of proving its righteousness. Has this truth about the futility of works of the law penetrated your heart and become a part of the fabric of your spiritual life? Where is your confidence in your spiritual life?

_____

_____

_____

Chapter 5—The Father's Cross

1. "Why did God become a human being? So that God as a human being might do and accomplish and achieve and complete all this for us wrongdoers, in order that in this way there might be brought about by him our reconciliation with him, and our conversion to him" (Barth, quoted in *Embracing God as Father*).[1] Spend some time meditating on God's purpose in the incarnation and all that he did to bring you to salvation.

_____

_____

_____

2. What does it tell you about God that he desired to reconcile the world to himself?

_____

_____

_____

3. Due to their profound impact on us, it can be difficult to achieve a balanced view of our parents, rightly appreciating their strength of character and also seeing their weaknesses. How does your experience of your parents' love affect your view of God? If you are a parent now, how has your experience of God as your Father impacted the way you seek to parent your child(ren)?

_____

_____

_____

_____

4. "[T]he cross is first and foremost a work of God *himself for himself*" (*Embracing God as Father*, 67). Is this a different idea from what you were taught about the cross? How does it affect your understanding to see it in the way described above?

_____

_____

_____

_____

5. "The cross is therefore an utter anomaly, a complete reversal of everything expected. ... Human reason simply can't grasp the depth of the wonder or even the irony in all this" (*Embracing God as Father*, 69-70). In *The Lion, the Witch, and the Wardrobe*, C. S. Lewis described the death of Aslan (the Christ figure in the story) like this: "When a willing victim who had committed no treachery was killed in a traitor's stead, the Great Stone Table would crack and Death itself would start working backward." Think of the ways that you have seen this worked out in your life.

_____

_____

_____

_____

6. The second part of Handel's *Messiah* (beginning with "Behold, the Lamb of God") is a wonderful aid to meditation on Christ's experience on the cross. The combination of words and music bring out the passion behind the story. What we often describe as Christ's passion is an outworking of God's passion to see his people rescued. Does the discussion of the Father's heart in this chapter change your perceptions about the crucifixion? If so, how so?

_____

_____

_____

_____

7. "[I]t would be ungracious, if he came forgiving man and yet laying more stress on what it cost Him to do it than His joy, fullness, and freedom in doing it" (Forsyth, quoted in *Embracing God as Father*).[2] How has experiencing God's grace changed the way you relate to those who fail you? Do you show them grace with the same attitude that God had in offering you grace?

_____

_____

_____

Chapter 6—Freed to Rest

1. What images come to your mind when you think about the word "rest"? What about "freed"?

_____

_____

_____

2. "It's bondage to a life of continual strife and struggle, a life filled with anxiety, defensiveness, competition, and animosity" (*Embracing God as Father*, 77). What effects of sin have you felt in your life? How have you struggled against these effects?

_____

_____

3. The exodus gives us a picture of how God works to rescue his people from bondage (as noted in this chapter). Write out the story of your conversion in terms of the exodus. How did God come to you? What did He do or show you that led you to trust Him? How did you finally leave your bondage behind and follow God to freedom?

_____

_____

4. How have you incorporated the Sabbath principle into your spiritual life? Where and when do you find rest?

_____

_____

_____

5. "Too much of our lives is just like that. We don't see each other; we don't see others as people to whom Christ came to bring freedom and rest" (*Embracing God as Father*, 79). How has the gospel changed the way you see the people around you? What things do you notice first about people—appearance, behavior, or how they show a need to know God?

_____

_____

_____

_____

6. "The Pharisees patrolled the boundaries of the Sabbath, watching like hawks to see who was in bounds and who wasn't" (*Embracing God as Father*, 80). What is it that makes this type of watching over people so tempting to us? How do you overcome that temptation?

_____

_____

_____

7. "What God gives by grace as a blessing, we turn into a means by which to earn his favor and lord it over others" (*Embracing God as Father*, 82). What gifts are you most frequently tempted to use as a means of measuring yourself? (Usually we pick things that come easily for us to use as a gauge of our performance.)

_____

_____

_____

8. "If you see yourself as a worn-out slave to expectations you're constantly failing to live up to, then you're not living in light of the reality of freedom and rest that belong to the Father's children. Do bondage to sin and an absence of peace characterize you? If so, as uncomfortable as it may be, ask yourself: Have I really grasped the gospel?" (*Embracing God as Father*, 82). The things mentioned in this quote are good indicators of your spiritual condition. Take some time to reflect and evaluate where you are with God.

_____

_____

_____

9. How do you see the two aspects of rest (described in this chapter) functioning in your life?

_____

_____

_____

10. "[T]he true test of a Christian is his or her reaction to life" (*Embracing God as Father*, 84). How do your reactions to events in your life show that you have experienced God's deliverance and that you are resting in him by faith?

_____

_____

_____

Chapter 7—Being in the Spirit

1. Look over your life. Is there more evidence that you are living according to the sinful nature or according to rest in the Father?

_____

_____

_____

2. Critical tones of voice and facial expressions can be deeply ingrained habits, and the fleshly tendency to justify them at times can leave them embedded in our lives. What other habits do you struggle with? What would a genuinely other-centered response look like in place of these habits?

_____

_____

_____

3. "The dominion of the flesh told you that you were related to God on the basis of what you do" (*Embracing God as Father*, 90). This is the theology to which the human heart naturally clings. Why do you think that is? How hard is it for you to let go of this perspective?

_____

_____

_____

4. "But the dominion of the Spirit tells you that you are related to God on the basis of what he did—by faith, you stand in Christ" (*Embracing God as Father*, 90). How long has it taken you to embrace this gospel truth? How has it become part of your life?

_____

_____

_____

5. "[T]he battle of faith ... [is] to believe that where God has said you are is actually where you are" (*Embracing God as Father*, 92). A continuing challenge for Christians is to believe what God has said instead of relying on their own assessment of their situation. How have you overcome this temptation?

_____

_____

_____

6. "You know who you are by faith, because the Spirit bears witness with your spirit that you are indeed sons and daughters of God, that your sonship is true" (*Embracing God as Father*, 93). Many Christians find that looking back over the course of their spiritual lives helps them to see how God has been at work. Here again, the Spirit bears witness to the truth of their status as sons and daughters of God. Take some time to review your spiritual life and make a list of the experiences that speak to the truth of your sonship.

_____

_____

_____

7. "Knowing who we are in Christ, finding our significance and security in the truth of his love for us, is the bedrock of our hope" (*Embracing God as Father*, 94). Learning to root our very identity in who we are in Christ is a key step for us as Christians. What obstacles stand in your way as you try to learn this? What other things in your life are you prone to measure your significance by?

_____

_____

_____

8. "[N]either death nor life, nor angels nor rulers, nor things present nor things to come, nor powers, nor height nor depth, nor anything else in all creation, will be able to separate us from the love of God in Christ Jesus our Lord" (Rom 8:38–39). Write these verses down on a card that you can carry with you, or post it somewhere you will see it multiple times daily as an aid to reflecting on this fundamental truth of the Christian life.

_____

_____

_____

Chapter 8—Walking in the Spirit

1. "God intimately makes his home in our hearts, filling them with his presence" (*Embracing God as Father*, 100). If you could maintain constant awareness of this fact, how do you think it would affect the way you act?

_____

_____

_____

2. "But nothing within God needs to be filled; he's already complete and therefore free of need" (*Embracing God as Father*, 100). How would your life be different if you were free from all your needs? What do you usually think of when you hear about "freedom in Christ"?

_____

_____

_____

_____

3. How have you used the law of God in your Christian life? Do you feel threatened by the demands of the law when you fail to live up to them? If so, how does the truth of the gospel change that?

_____

_____

_____

_____

4. "Yet striving after obedience to the law doesn't make us holy. 'For by works of the law no human being will be justified in [God's] sight' (Rom 3:20)" (*Embracing God as Father*, 101). If a stranger observed your life very closely for a week, would he conclude that you believe this?

_____

_____

_____

5. Reread the descriptions of the "happy moralist" and the "sad moralist." Which one better describes you? Make a list of the ways you show that tendency.

_____

_____

_____

_____

6. "Though I often confessed to God that I, of course, deserved nothing, yet still I harbored a secret hope of recommending myself to God by all these duties and all this morality. In other words, I healed myself with my duties" (David Brainerd, quoted in *Embracing God as Father*).[1] Can you relate to this account? When have you been most prone to working to "heal yourself"?

_____

_____

_____

7. "Therefore, if anyone is in Christ, he is a new creation. The old has passed away; behold, the new has come" (2 Cor 5:17). Take a moment to think back over your spiritual life. When did you become new creation? What makes you feel most like a new creation?

_____

_____

_____

8. "There is no power whatsoever in our fleshly will to walk like this" (*Embracing God as Father*, 107). In what ways have you tried to walk in these ways by your own strength? How has that worked out in your life? Do you believe the quote is true?

_____

_____

_____

9. "Put differently, we don't fully believe that he sees us, that he cares for us, that he is leading us, that he is defending us, that he is providing for us, that he is the single answer to all we need" (*Embracing God as Father*, 108). How would you rate your comprehension of God's love for you? Do those around you see evidence in your life that you believe God loves you? How does it show in your interactions with people in your life?

_____

_____

_____

10. A common misunderstanding of the gospel is that God for-
gives your sins, but you then need to earn his favor by your own
righteousness (see description in this chapter). How does the
true gospel message relieve the burden of such thinking? Have
you believed the true gospel and lost that burden?

_____

_____

_____

Chapter 9—Confident Access

1. The title of this chapter is "Confident Access." Take some time to consider how access to God has played out as a theme throughout the history of God's people. Adam and Eve enjoyed intimate access to God in the garden of Eden (Gen 2). But this access was lost in the fall, and consequently sinful men and women began to fear God's presence (Exod 20:19). The work of Christ made it possible for God's people to be restored to a place in God's household. How do you think about your spiritual life in terms of access to God?

_____

_____

_____

_____

2. Consider "God's eternal plan to bestow spiritual blessing through adopting us into Jesus Christ" (*Embracing God as Father*, 113). What we know of adoption gives us a realistic picture in the physical world of what our adoption in Christ does for us in the spiritual realm. Think of the most compelling and moving story you have heard of someone adopting a child from disadvantaged (or even desperate) circumstances. How does it compare to God adopting you in Christ? Is it hard for you to think of yourself as spiritually helpless, as a child in need of adoption?

_____

_____

_____

_____

3. The divide between Jew and Gentile was literally a separation of God's chosen people from all others. Paul lists the advantages the Jews had in Romans 9:4-5. The Gentiles (literally, all the other nations of the world) were cut off from these benefits. How does it feel to have this barrier broken down for you? What are you doing to let others know it has been broken down?

_____

_____

_____

4. "God adopts us out of His free love, not because our character and record shows us worthy to bear his name, but despite the fact that they show the opposite" (J. I. Packer, *Knowing God*).[1] Worthiness is not a trait that is usually evaluated in a young child in need of adoption, but considering our unworthiness adds a dimension to our understanding of what God has done in adopting us. Can you think of an analogy that closely reflects God's adoption of unworthy sinners into his family?

_____

_____

_____

5. Psalm 91 give beautiful expression to the idea of God as our protector. Take time to read and meditate on it this week.

_____

_____

_____

6. "There are no distinctions of affection in the divine family. We are all loved just as fully as Jesus is loved" (J. I. Packer, *Knowing God*).[2] Think about your experience within your own family. Were there (or did there appear to be) distinctions of affection? How hard is it for you to grasp that God loves you as fully as he does Jesus? Take time to express your feelings about this to him.

_____

_____

_____

7. The requirements which the high priest had to fulfill on the Day of Atonement in order to enter into the holy of holies are elaborate and onerous (see Lev 16). When you consider these requirements and the fact that you now have access into the presence of God, what does it tell you about how much Christ accomplished for you?

_____

_____

_____

8. "Since your access to God isn't based on what you do but wholly based on what Christ has done, it can't be lost" (*Embracing God as Father*, 119). Do your failures ever make you feel that God has moved away from you because of what you've done? Are you convinced that this is not true? What can you do to change the way you respond to your failures?

_____

_____

_____

9. "No matter how we feel, we remain a son or daughter of the Father because of his love for us in Christ (John 3:16–17)" (*Embracing God as Father*, 120). It is often difficult to root our feelings about ourselves in the truth of God's word instead of in our own understanding and experience. What will you do to more firmly ground your identity in what God says about you?

_____

_____

_____

Chapter 10—Joyful Mission

1. "Both sons were lost; their 'lost-ness' is merely expressed differently. The younger brother's rebellion was conspicuous, the elder brother's concealed" (*Embracing God as Father*, 123). Is the idea that both sons were lost new to you? Which brother are you more similar to?

_____

_____

_____

2. "He joyfully received and feasted with sinners (Luke 15:1–3) *because this is how the heart of the eternal Father* receives his wayward children" (*Embracing God as Father*, 123). How far has this attitude of the Father penetrated your own heart? Do you rejoice to receive "sinners" as fellow sons and daughters of God?

_____

_____

_____

3. Which character's actions do you find the most scandalous—the father, younger brother, or elder brother? What does your answer say about how you see God and his love for sinners?

_____

_____

_____

4. To refresh your understanding of the kinsman-redeemer, read the book of Ruth (four chapters!) in the Old Testament. How did Jesus meet the requirements to be our *go'el*: a blood relative of the one in need, free (i.e., not in the same need of redemption), willing to act in the capacity, and able to pay the redemption?

_____

_____

5. The younger son's plan for going home (taking the lesser position of a hired worker) indicates he also believed he should in some way pay for his mistakes and earn his way back into the father's favor. How does the father's welcome undercut this common response (by both the wayward and their observers)? Is the younger son's plan realistic (i.e., could the wages of a hired man pay back the share of the estate the younger son had spent)? How is that similar to our situation with God?

_____

_____

_____

6. "[T]here's no greater joy than coming to the end of ourselves, weeping over our foolishness, and discovering that God doesn't leave us hungry and naked and exposed—he repeatedly runs with joy to cover our shame as we turn homeward" (*Embracing God as Father*, 128). Have you ever felt that your shame was too great to be covered by God, or that would run out of patience with the amount of shame that you have? How does seeing the father's welcome of the younger son change your understanding of how God feels toward you?

_____

_____

7. "The mutual love of the Father and Son is oriented wholly away from self and towards the other" (*Embracing God as Father*, 129). Have you ever experienced love from someone that felt wholly directed towards you? Have you ever felt love for another that seemed wholly directed towards that person? Who was the person and what were the circumstances?

_____

_____

_____

8. "God's holiness isn't a passive and stoic flawlessness but an activeness in which he makes certain no separation exists between him and his beloved" (*Embracing God as Father*, 130). How does this compare with your understanding of God's holiness? How does this change the way you feel about God?

_____

_____

_____

9. "They see the depth of their own sin and the greater depth of the Father's inviting holiness. Jesus said, 'He who is forgiven little, loves little' (Luke 7:47)" (*Embracing God as Father*, 130). How much have you been forgiven? How has that affected how much love you feel for God and for those around you?

_____

_____

_____

10. Jesus' encounter with the Samaritan woman at the well gives us a wonderful picture of how God works: his Son seeking out and saving lost sinners so that they may worship the Father in truth. Write out how God sought you and brought you into his family.

_____

_____

_____

11. Reread Zephaniah 3:15, 17, quoted at the end of this chapter. How hard is it for you to believe that God rejoices over you with singing? Remember that his rejoicing is not rooted in what you have done or not done, but in what Jesus did for you so that God would accept you.

_____

_____

_____

Chapter 11—Perfecting Sons and Daughters

1. What does "discipline" mean to you? What images come to mind when you think about discipline? With regard to your spiritual life, how have you used discipline in the past? Did your discipline focus on changing your behavior?

_____

_____

_____

2. The human heart naturally assumes that a *quid pro quo* exists with regard to the good events and bad events that come into our lives: Those who do good things get good things; those who do bad things get bad things. Jesus' disciples had the same idea (see John 9:1-3). How have you looked at the good and bad things that come into your life? Have you felt responsible in some way when you have suffered? Who did you think was responsible for blessings and prosperity in your life?

_____

_____

_____

3. How easy is it for you to trust God's purposes when you suffer? Can you think of a difficult time in your life when you struggled to trust God, but now you can see that he brought good things out of it? Do you sometimes wonder why you have suffered more or less than some you know?

_____

_____

_____

4. "His appetite for the Father was stronger than his appetite for a pain-free existence, and this carried him to the cross" (*Embracing God as Father*, 137). How strong is your appetite for the Father? Is it stronger than your appetite for a pain-free existence? What else do you have an appetite for that rivals your appetite for the Father?

_____

_____

_____

5. "Divine discipline isn't meant to herd us to where we're not, but to confirm where we are" (*Embracing God as Father*, 138). How does this statement fit with what you have thought about discipline for most of your Christian life?

_____

_____

_____

6. "For when behavioral conformity is made primary, discipline becomes punishment. It is a quick step from this to the assumption that behavior is what wins or loses God's approval and gains his blessing or punishment" (*Embracing God as Father*, 138). How does this statement compare with your experience with discipline in your life (growing up and/or in your spiritual life)? How have you been able to change this natural orientation of the human heart?

_____

_____

_____

7. "[Earthly discipline] doesn't, however, regenerate the heart and promote a passion for trusting God because it leaves untouched our passion for self and self-trust—it doesn't touch the heart" (*Embracing God as Father*, 139). How deep is *your* "passion for self and self-trust"? Do you recognize when you are trying to please God by performing in your own strength? How has God begun to change you in this area?

_____

_____

_____

8. The New Testament writers used two different words for punishment and discipline. How does that affect the way you think about how God uses suffering in the lives of his children? Will this help you trust God in times of suffering?

_____

_____

_____

9. "They all matured through suffering, through which they learned to trust God—to attend to his promises more than their failures and the inadequacy of their circumstances" (*Embracing God as Father*, 141). If you believe this, then how important is it to know God's promises from his Word? What is the biggest help to you in trusting God's promise more than your circumstances? What is the biggest challenge?

_____

_____

_____

10. Read the quote from P. T. Forsyth in this chapter (p. 142). He seems to list everything that Christians prefer to focus on instead of trusting God. Which of the things are you most prone to stress in your spiritual life? Do you accept his conclusion?

_____

_____

_____

Chapter 12—The United Family

1. "It's impossible to overstate the importance of unity. Teams, parties, boards, and marriages function poorly without it" (*Embracing God as Father*, 144). Think of the various situations you've been in where unity was sought and stressed as important. How did it feel to be in those groups? How long did that unity last?

_____

_____

_____

"Unity and uniformity are thereby conflated, so to speak with a different voice threatens the status quo" (*Embracing God as Father*, 146). Does that statement resonate with you because of your experiences? How would you describe the issues that led to the desire for uniformity and not just unity?

_____

_____

_____

2. "In other words, the more the church is focused on God, as opposed to itself, the more openhearted and loving it becomes" (*Embracing God as Father*, 146). How do the churches that you know compare with this statement? How would you describe the most openhearted church you've been in?

_____

_____

_____

3. "The more we are filled with the Holy Spirit, as opposed to self, the more Christ's love overflows through us" (*Embracing God as Father*, 146). How have you seen this principle at work in your life? Would people who know you say they have seen the results in your life?

_____

_____

_____

_____

4. Take time to read through Psalms 120–134. What images stand out to you as you read these songs of ascent?

_____

_____

_____

_____

5. Read Psalm 133 (*Embracing God as Father*, 147–48). What do the two images tell you about unity? Which image in the psalm is more compelling to you, the fragrant anointing oil or the dew of Mount Hermon?

_____

_____

_____

_____

6. "Like orphans abandoned to the city streets, we very often think and act as if this is the only life" (*Embracing God as Father*, 149). When in your life has that been true of you? How do you keep eternity in mind as you live each day?

---

7. "This means true Christian community is community in and through Christ alone, not through coercion, carrots, or cravings. It might come as a shock, but merely gathering in a church building doesn't constitute Christian community—it can actually be, at times, the farthest thing from Christian community" (*Embracing God as Father*, 150–51). How well does this match your experience? Where and when have you best experienced Christian community?

---

8. "What persons are in themselves as Christians, in their inwardness and piety, cannot constitute the basis of our community, which is determined by what those persons are in terms of Christ. Our community consists solely in what Christ has done to both of us" (Bonhoeffer, *Life Together*).[1] How does this idea challenge your approach to community? How well do you relate to Christians who are very different from you?

---

9. "Our unity in Christ is greater than our ability to conceive it. Yet, paradoxically, both joy and grief testify to it, and both of these come from the Spirit of God" (*Embracing God as Father*, 152). Does this statement surprise you? Have you experienced both joy and grief because of the unity in Christ that you have with other believers? Read the discussion of joy and grief in the section called "Greater Than Conceived." How will this understanding affect your experience of joy and grief within Christian community?

_____

_____

_____

10. "Transformation occurs as our gaze lingers on the face of Jesus turned towards us" (*Embracing God as Father*, 154). How does this fit with your understanding of how transformation happens in your spiritual life? Do you expect to experience transformation without putting in a lot of effort?

_____

_____

_____

Afterword

1. "More than ever before, we see that the Christian life consists not of a set of theological formulae or pietistic techniques, left in our hands to apply, but trust!" (*Embracing God as Father*, 158). How has this book changed your reaction to this statement? Do you want faith and trust to be the mainstays of your Christian life?

_____

_____

_____

2. "We are sons and daughters, the children of hope, in a cynical and despairing hour" (*Embracing God as Father*, 159). How has this book changed the way you see God as your father? How will this affect the hope that you have for your life and the future?

_____

_____

_____

Notes

Introduction

1. G. C. Bingham, "Ah Strong, Strong Love," *New Creation Hymn Book*, No. 30 (Blackwood: New Creation Publications, n.d.).

2. Thomas Chalmers, *The Expulsive Power of a New Affection* (1855; repr., Minneapolis: Curiosmith, 2012), 28–29.

Chapter 2—Filled with Fullness

1. C. Whittaker, *Great Revivals: God's Men and Their Message* (Basingstoke: Marshall Pickering, 1984), 160.

2. Martin Luther, *Luther's Works*, Vol. 27 (ed. J. Pelikan; St. Louis: Concordia Publishing House, 1963), 35.

Chapter 3—The Father's Plan

1. This passage of Luther is widely quoted, and appears in the Weimar Edition of *Luther's Works*, Vol. 54 (1928), 86. This citation is found in F. F. Bruce, *Paul: Apostle of the Heart Set Free* (Grand Rapids: Eerdmans, 1977), 471.

2. Kirsten Buchanan, "No. 425," *New Creation Hymn Book* (2d ed.; Blackwood: New Creation Publications, 2010).

3. George Smeaton, *The Apostles' Doctrine of the Atonement* (Edinburgh: T & T Clark, 1870), 307–08.

Chapter 4—The Lord in Our Midst

1. For an excellent exploration of this idea, see Helmut Thielicke, *Between God and Satan: The Temptations of Jesus and the Temptability of Man* (Farmington Hills, MI: Oil Lamp Books, 2010).
2. Dietrich Bonhoeffer, *Life Together* (New York: HarperCollins, 1954), 23 (echoing Luther's comments on Galatians 6:1–4).

Chapter 5—The Father's Cross

1. Karl Barth, *Church Dogmatics* (IV/1; Edinburgh: T & T Clark), 222.
2. P. T. Forsyth, "God the Holy Father," in *God the Holy Father* (1957; repr., Blackwood: New Creation Publications, 1987), 19.
3. C. H. Spurgeon, "Living, Loving, Lasting Union" (funeral address delivered 22 October 1890).
4. P. T. Forsyth, "God the Holy Father," 17.

Chapter 7—Being in the Spirit

1. William H. Goold, ed., *The Works of John Owen,* Vol. 7 (Edinburgh: Banner of Truth, 1965), 520.
2. Martin Luther, *Heidelberg Disputation,* Thesis 26.

Chapter 8—Walking in the Spirit

1. We are indebted to Elyse Fitzpatrick and Dennis Johnson's book, *Counsel from the Cross: Connecting Broken People to the Love of Christ* (Wheaton: Crossway, 2009), 73–81, for their description of the happy and sad moralists and related quotations.
2. Martin Luther, *Luther's Works,* Vol. 42 (ed. Jaroslav Pelikan and Helmut T. Lehmann; Philadelphia: Fortress, 1958–1972), 7–14.
3. George Whitefield, "The Method of Grace," *The World's Famous Orations* (ed. William Jennings Bryan and Francis W. Halsey; New York: Funk and Wagnalls Company, 1906), n.p. Online: http://www.bartleby. com/268/3/20.
4. Distilled from Jonathan Edwards, David Brainerd, and Sereno Edwards Dwight, *The Works of Presented Edwards with a Memoir of His Life* (New York: G. & C. & H. Carvill, 1830), 36, 38, 43.
5. C. H. Spurgeon, *Treasury of the New Testament,* Vol. 4 (London: Marshall, Morgan & Scott, c. 1934), 554.

Chapter 9—Confident Access

1. J. I. Packer, *Knowing God* (Downers Grove, Ill: InterVarsity Press, 1973), 195.
2. Packer, *Knowing God,* 196.

3. Helmut Thielicke, *Being Human...Becoming Human: An Essay in Christian Anthropology*, (trans. Geoffrey W. Bromiley; New York: Doubleday, 1984), 96–97.
4. Helmut Thielicke, *Being Human...Becoming Human*, 135.

Chapter 10—Joyful Mission

1. For excellent cultural background, see K. Bailey, *The Cross and the Prodigal: Luke 15 Through the Eyes of Middle Eastern Peasants* (Downers Grove: InterVarsity Press, 2005), and K. Bailey, *Poet and Peasant and Through Peasant Eyes: A Literary-Cultural Approach to the Parables in Luke*, combined edition (Grand Rapids: Eerdmans, 1976).
2. Martin Luther, *Luther's Works*, Vol. 26 (ed. J. Pelikan; St. Louis: Concordia, 1963), 389.
3. Martin Luther, *Luther's Works*, Vol. 27, 111.

Chapter 11—Perfecting Sons and Daughters

1. Thomas Chalmers, "The Expulsive Power of a New Affection." For further exploration of the four summary passions of the heart, see Larry Crabb, *The Safest Place on Earth* (Nashville: Thomas Nelson, 1999), 81–94.
2. P. T. Forsyth, "Christian Perfection," in *God the Holy Father* (1957; repr., Blackwood: New Creation Publications, 1987), 126–27.

Chapter 12—The United Family

1. Tomas Halik, *Patience with God: The Story of Zacchaeus Continuing in Us* (trans. Gerald Turner; New York: Doubleday, 2009), x.
2. Taken from the Lutheran authorized form.
3. Dietrich Bonhoeffer, *Life Together: Prayerbook of the Bible* (Vol. 5 of *Dietrich Bonhoeffer Works*; ed. Wayne Whitson Floyd, Jr.; Minneapolis: Augsburg Fortress, 1996), 34–35.
4. Helmut Thielicke, *Foundations* (Vol. 1 of *Theological Ethics*; ed. William H. Lazareth; Grand Rapids: Eerdmans, 1979), 181.
5. Geoffrey Bingham, "One Day We'll See Him Face to Face," *New Creation Hymn Book*, No. 183 (Blackwood: New Creation Publications, 1986).

Study Guide: Introduction

1. Thomas Chalmers, *The Expulsive Power of a New Affection* (1855; repr., Minneapolis: Curiosmith, 2012), 28–29; quoted in Bush and Due, *Embracing God as Father*, 8.

Study Guide: Chapter 2

1. Martin Luther, *Luther's Works*, Vol. 27 (ed. J. Pelikan; St. Louis: Concordia Publishing House, 1963), 35; quoted in Bush and Due, *Embracing God as Father*, 31.

Study Guide: Chapter 3

1. Weimar Edition of *Luther's Works,* Vol. 54 (1928), 86. This citation is found in F. F. Bruce, *Paul: Apostle of the Heart Set Free* (Grand Rapids: Eerdmans, 1977), 471; quoted in Bush and Due, *Embracing God as Father*, 35.

Study Guide: Chapter 5

1. Karl Barth, *Church Dogmatics* (IV/1; Edinburgh: T & T Clark), 222; quoted in Bush and Due, *Embracing God as Father*, 64.

2. P. T. Forsyth, "God the Holy Father," in *God the Holy Father* (1957; repr., Blackwood: New Creation Publications, 1987), 17; quoted in Bush and Due, *Embracing God as Father*, 71.

Study Guide: Chapter 8

1. Distilled from Jonathan Edwards, David Brainerd, and Sereno Edwards Dwight, *The Works of Presented Edwards with a Memoir of His Life* (New York: G. & C. & H. Carvill, 1830), 36, 38, 43; quoted in Bush and Due, *Embracing God as Father*, 104–05.

Study Guide: Chapter 9

1. J. I. Packer, *Knowing God* (Downers Grove, Ill: InterVarsity Press, 1973), 195; quoted in Bush and Due, *Embracing God as Father*, 114.

2. Packer, *Knowing God*, 196; quoted in Bush and Due, *Embracing God as Father*, 116.

Study Guide: Chapter 12

1. Dietrich Bonhoeffer, *Life Together: Prayerbook of the Bible* (Vol. 5 of *Dietrich Bonhoeffer Works*; ed. Wayne Whitson Floyd, Jr.; Minneapolis: Augsburg Fortress, 1996), 34–35; quoted in Bush and Due, *Embracing God as Father*, 151.

Subject and Author Index

Scripture Index

Old Testament

About the Authors

Daniel Bush (Ph.D., University of Aberdeen, Scotland) is a pastor in the Evangelical Presbyterian Church. He is author, also with Noel Due, of *Live in Liberty: The Spiritual Message of Galatians.*

Noel Due (D.Min., Reformed Theological Seminary, Jackson) is a regional resourcing pastor for the Lutheran Church of Australia based in Cairns, Queensland. He has ministered as a pastor, lecturer, and conference speaker for more than 25 years.

Steve W. Brown (Litt.D., King College) is one of the most sought-after preachers and conference speakers in the United States. In addition to extensive radio and pastoral experience, he currently is heard on national radio program *Key Life* and serves as visiting professor of practical theology at Knox Theological Seminary. Steve is the author of numerous books, including *A Scandalous Freedom, What Was I Thinking?, Approaching God,* and *Three Free Sins.* He also serves on the Board of the National Religious Broadcasters and Harvest USA.

Lee Beckham (M.Sci., Georgia Institute of Technology) has over 25 years of lay ministry experience with churches, campus ministries, and military Christian fellowships. For over 14 years, he has served as a ruling elder at Alexandria Presbyterian Church in Alexandria, Virginia, with responsibilities in administration, evangelism, missions, and lay counseling.

Explore the Gospel in Galatians

A systemic problem plagues the local and global church: We habitually lose the gospel. In its place, we substitute personal prosperity, legalism, politics—and we end up paralyzing the mission of the church. In *Live in Liberty*, Daniel Bush and Noel Due examine Paul's passionate defense of the gospel in Galatians, showing us how to enjoy God's presence and everlasting peace, setting us free to love and be loved.

Visit **LexhamPress.com/liberty** to learn more.

Discover the Depths of God's Grace

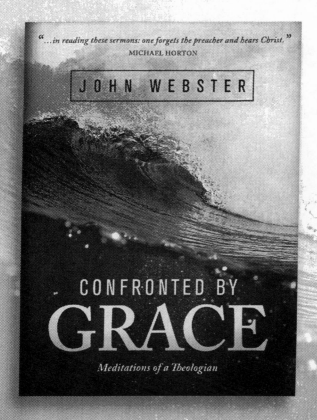

This rich collection of thoughtful sermons from a leading theologian is challenging, stimulating, and inspiring. Born from years of study, these reflections demonstrate the complexity of the Christian life and the depth of the grace of God. *Confronted by Grace* points us toward Christ so that we may grow in our understanding of the truth of the gospel.

Visit **LexhamPress.com/confronted** to learn more.